States of Plague

States of Plague

READING ALBERT CAMUS IN A PANDEMIC

Alice Kaplan & Laura Marris

The University of Chicago Press

CHICAGO AND LONDON

The University of Chicago Press, Chicago 60637
The University of Chicago Press, Ltd., London
© 2022 by Alice Kaplan and Laura Marris
Published 2022
Paperback edition 2024
Printed in the United States of America

33 32 31 30 29 28 27 26 25 24   1 2 3 4 5

ISBN-13: 978-0-226-81553-4 (cloth)
ISBN-13: 978-0-226-83330-9 (paper)
ISBN-13: 978-0-226-81554-1 (e-book)
DOI: https://doi.org/10.7208/chicago/9780226815541.001.0001

Library of Congress Cataloging-in-Publication Data

Names: Kaplan, Alice Yaeger, author. | Marris, Laura, 1987– author.
Title: States of plague : reading Albert Camus in a pandemic / Alice
    Kaplan and Laura Marris.
Description: Chicago : University of Chicago Press, 2022. | Includes
    bibliographical references and index.
Identifiers: LCCN 2021061982 | ISBN 9780226815534 (cloth) |
    ISBN 9780226815541 (ebook)
Subjects: LCSH: Camus, Albert, 1913–1960. Peste. | Epidemics in
    literature. | COVID-19 Pandemic, 2020–
Classification: LCC PQ2605.A3734 P4358 2022 | DDC 843/.914—dc23/
    eng/20220107
LC record available at https://lccn.loc.gov/2021061982

♾ This paper meets the requirements of ANSI/NISO Z39.48-1992
(Permanence of Paper).

The day the number of deaths once again reached thirty, Bernard Rieux looked at the official cable that the prefect had handed him, saying, "They got scared." The cable read: "Declare a state of plague. Close the city."

ALBERT CAMUS, *The Plague*

CONTENTS

PREFACE

Camus originally intended his novel as an allegory of World War II. But every allegory has a collapse point where truth undoes the figure. As readers who worked with *The Plague* during a pandemic year, we wondered how Camus could know so much about what we were living through: the official denials, the bureaucracy, the numbness, the end of travel, the monotony of waiting, and especially our separation from one another. We conceived *States of Plague* in response, imagining our book as a guide to these moments where the written and the real collide.

Through a strange coincidence, the city of Oran, where Camus set *The Plague*, was one of the last places we visited before the outbreak of COVID forced many borders to close. We had traveled to Algeria together to research the sites of the book and to lead a seminar on Camus. At the time, Alice was introducing new editions of his personal and committed writings and teaching *The Plague* at Yale. Laura had begun a new translation of the novel for A. A. Knopf. We didn't yet know how much more immersed we were about to become.

When it was originally published in 1947, critics immediately recognized their own world in *The Plague*. An early reviewer said there was no mistaking it: "The plague is obviously the Brown Plague, Nazism, the universe of the camps." Camus acknowledged that the Occupation was one "key" to his allegory: "*The Plague*, which I wanted to work on several levels, has as its obvious content the struggle of a European resistance against Nazism."[1] Those were his intentions. During COVID-19, that reading tradition was transformed, in part because of how sharply Camus portrays disease and transmission. For those who came to the novel in a pandemic, the subject of the allegory was closer than the war Camus had intended to represent.

Unhinged from allegory, the plot works directly: *The Plague* takes place in Oran, where a mysterious illness is killing the rats. Soon, humans begin to fall sick as well, and though the politicians do not want to admit that a crisis is happening, the city quickly realizes a full-blown epidemic is at hand. Before long, Oran is under quarantine, and its residents have to figure out how to face the disease and survive the suffering it brings.

Camus's chronicle of events follows Dr. Rieux, a modest, direct man who quickly realizes that he has been confronted with extraordinary circumstances. Separated from his wife who has left the city, Rieux fights the plague as best he can while hoping that one of his colleagues will be able to develop a serum. The cure is slow in coming, and the city government is hesitant to roll out preventative measures, leading to a rapid rise in cases.

For many people, *The Plague* feels personal now. Over the last year, we've heard from readers who began to see it as a book about their own lives—a book with insight into the experience of a global health crisis. And through this lens, certain features became vital: Camus's sensitivity toward illness, his experience of a contagious disease, the cost of separation in his own life, and the psychology and politics of the city in quarantine. In writing these pieces, we were working to hold the past and present of *The Plague* in conversation—to recognize how the novel has reached people in our current moment, and to consider its tangled literary history.

In these pages, we've allowed the uncertain experience of the past year to refract through our experience of reading—to mark how this novel was closer to our own environment than we might have wanted to admit. Every Sunday during the months of lockdown, we discussed the ways these essays were arranging themselves in our minds. These calls between Paris and New Haven and Buffalo became a respite, an antidote to the confines of our cities, a monthslong conversation that made working with *The Plague* less lonely. Because we come to the book from different perspectives, we wanted to see what would happen if we alternated between them, so that our chapters could offer two contrasting ways of looking. Alice's essays engage the forces of history, while Laura's are drawn to the ecology of landscape and language. At the top of each chapter, we've noted our pieces by name. Of course, our proclivities as readers overlapped as we learned from each other, and as our sense of Camus evolved under the force of a new reality, alongside the pressures of illness, recovery, concern, and care in our own lives.

In this undertaking, we've been fortunate. If we hadn't been to Algeria just before the pandemic began, the research for this book would not have been possible. We're especially grateful to the people who shared their knowledge of Oran and Algeria with us, including Abdeslem Abdelhak, Sarah Bouchakour, Walid Bouchakour, Ameziane Ferhani, Pierre Gillon, Djamel Hachi, Sofiane Hadjadj, Selma Hellal, Elisabeth Leuvrey, Père Guillaume Michel, Gabriel Rosenzweig, Samir Toumi, and Grégor Trumel.

During the months we were writing, our world crept up on allegory, changing its resonances, making it seem true. Passages that might once have seemed artful now spoke directly to our own fear and grief. We learned to look at the skies of a plague spring, to examine the body politic and the politics of immunity. And to consider how artists imagine and reinvent the world during a crisis, drawing back the veil on other possible futures. This novel wasn't an easy text to work with—a brutal yet hopeful companion. While *The Plague* was in our lives long before the pandemic, there are accidents of timing that change your reading forever.

States of Plague

1 WE, DR. RIEUX

Alice

I imagine a chronicle that would begin: "day 20 of COVID," in which I claim my disease in medias res. I joke with Laura that after being sick, I'll never write about Camus's novel the same way. In fact, I'm worried that the effort of getting through this illness is making me indifferent to writing about it. But I end up typing in a daze, drawn to the words in spite of myself. The doctor said to watch out for day seven: that's when some people dive deeper into violent illness. If my oxygen rate falls below 94, I should call "15" for an ambulance. He's the neighborhood doctor I last saw for a special authorization to swim because of "skeletal problems," who gave me a fifty-euro *prix d'ami*—a discount for his swimming prescription. Now he's on the phone saying don't call me, there's nothing I'll be able to do. If I call "15," he says, an ambulance will take me to whatever hospital has beds left. Sure enough on day seven I get much worse. After a month, I'm still coughing—a disagreeable hack that doesn't respond to any lozenge or syrup.

Camus's novel, too, is a chronicle, but it isn't a personal account. That's the first thing I notice when I return to *The Plague*. Instead, it's a chronicle of events—a report of what happens from day to day as people deal with the plague. It's too polished to be a diary. This anonymous narrator doesn't want to name himself—he says "we" instead of "I." We do feel the narrator's fatigue, but it's the fatigue of an entire city.

It's worth looking at the passage where Camus sets up his narrator's secret:

> As for the narrator, whom you'll meet in due course, he would never have tried to put himself forward for this kind of undertaking if chance had not given him the opportunity to collect a certain number of accounts and if the force of things hadn't gotten him mixed up in all he presumes to relate. That's what authorized him to take on the historian's task. Of course, even if he's an amateur, a historian always has sources. The narrator of this story therefore has his own: first of all what he witnessed, then what others witnessed, since, through his role, he ended up collecting the secrets of everyone involved in this chronicle, and last, the texts which finally fell into his hands.[1]

It's pretty unusual in a novel to have a narrator who tells you he is not going to give away his identity. So what could be the advantage? Why did Camus decide to use a narrator who refuses to say his name?

For one thing, withholding the identity of the narrator is a sure way to give the book momentum, a clever tactic to create mystery and to make sure the reader turns the pages, hoping he'll be revealed. Modesty is key. The narrator explains that his identity will be known "in due course," that he won't give himself away. He's been authorized to tell the story by accident, by the force of things, and he's uncomfortable with the pressure of that responsibility. On American television, we hear about the heroes on the front lines, the people risking their lives. But in the novel, the refusal of heroism is key to Camus's values.

In December 1946, Camus wrote a letter to his friend Louis Guilloux, who had just read *The Plague* in manuscript. Camus reports that he's made all the revisions Guilloux suggested but that he's changed nothing about the narrator. Yet he realizes this business about the narrator is confusing. He reports that he's added a new sentence to the last chapter: "it's time to admit the narrator is none other than Bernard Rieux."[2] Camus explains to Guilloux that Rieux's suffering is shared with the suffering of other people—which is why he can remain objective—not focused on his particular story. "This is important to me," Camus writes to his friend. "It's the secret of the book, its power." He adds that if the device succeeds, readers will be compelled to reread the novel as soon as they've finished.

The *secret* of the novel. We know that the narrator has to be someone who writes—but the novel is full of writers! It could be Grand, an obsessional scribbler (although he has writer's block and keeps writing the same sentence over and over) It could be Rambert, a journalist (who would be used to writing chronicles), and of course it could be Tarrou, who is keeping his own private surreal journal of the plague, concentrating on insignificance.

The narrator reveals that he is "better placed" to speak about lovers,[3] but there are several people in the novel who are separated from their loved ones. Grand's wife left him fifteen years earlier. Rieux's wife is at a sanatorium. Rambert's wife is in Paris. A newspaper, the *Courier of the Epidemic*, is launched—to "inform our fellow citizens, with a care for scrupulous objectivity, of the rise and fall of the disease,"[4] but in fact the *Courier of the Epidemic* attempts to lure people with advertisements for products that promise to prevent plague. The paper is the unreliable narrator of the epidemic—the opposite of the unassuming but stalwart chronicler of the novel.

As the story progresses, Camus plants real clues and red herrings, and as characters die, you are forced to eliminate candidates for the role of narrator.

Fact about this narrator: he is able to recount the plague from many points of view, many neighborhoods. He bears witness to personal tragedies, like a private detective in a noir novel who has access to the scenes of a crime, or like the demon Asmodeus, who lifts the roofs off houses. Or, as we'll finally figure out, like a doctor who makes house calls, who can move from the business district to the hospital to the poorest neighborhoods of the city in an afternoon. Sometimes, through his movements, he almost gives himself away.

So there's the literary advantage—making the pages turn around a mystery—and the ethical advantage: Camus's commitment to an anonymous narrator is about making *The Plague* a story of more than one person's experience. Camus's first novel, *The Stranger*, is narrated in the first person by Meursault, although we know very little about what's going on in his mind. Camus plays with the conventions of first-person narrative: a character who says "I" but who is impenetrable, unlike in a standard autobiography where the "I" makes us feel close to the narrator. Meursault's flatness lends a strangeness to everything that transpires.

With *The Plague*, as Camus reflects on the experience of resistance, he plays with narrative convention once again, but this time his focus is the "we." What matters to him ethically is to create a *collective story*, the story of a community under oppression. He's anticipating a genre that Latin American writers will perfect, the *testimonio*, in the tradition of *I, Rigoberta Menchu*, the autobiography of an indigenous Guatemalan woman and a collective reckoning. "I'd like to stress that it's not only *my* life," she begins, "it's also the testimony of my people."[5] At the end of *The Plague*, Rieux explains: "Being called to testify, upon the occasion of a sort of crime, he has kept a certain reserve, as is appropriate for an honest witness."[6]

So the narrator's desire to remain anonymous is central to Camus's ethics . . . he wants his narrator to remain selfless for as long as possible; a kind of eye, with more than his own interests or particular story at heart. But in fact, everyone seems to want to write about the plague in a different way—Tarrou with his eccentric diary entries, Rieux through his letters to his wife, Grand by not writing about the plague at all but imagining a beautiful horse and rider in the Bois de Boulogne. As these possible narrators parade before our eyes, Camus gives us time to think about who best tells the story of the disaster, who is authorized.

Here in France, the panic everywhere reminds me of how important the basic questions of Camus's novel remain. Who is going to speak for the nation during a pandemic? Is there a universal narrator of a national situation? Should there be?

I find myself thinking about Camus's newspaper *Combat* and its postwar motto—"from resistance to revolution." By 1946, as he was perfecting his narrative strategy, *Combat* had been aboveground for two years. Articles were now signed, and stars were born, like the essayist and filmmaker Alexandre Astruc, and these writers went on to brilliant careers in the cultural sphere. Some people still used pseudonyms. Simone de Beauvoir for one, who reported from Portugal as "Daniel Secretan," obviously enjoying her secret.[7] But hiding your name was no longer a question of life and death, as it had been under the Occupation, when pseudonyms were a form of protection, and when you could be tortured by the Gestapo until you named the head of your Resistance cell.

The Plague's anonymous narrator and the displacement of war stories onto an epidemic served different functions. Camus was now giving the French the possibility of experiencing the trauma of the war at one layer's remove. In theory, more people could connect to a novel about a plague than a specific story from occupied France—a specific Resistance movement, or one convoy of Jews deported, or one group of Resistance fighters, or one village massacred by the SS. In *The Plague*, Camus could point to many wartime experiences at once: to many martyrs, many acts of resistance and cowardice. Everyone in France had a war story, and Camus's novel became an echo chamber for these narratives.

A paradox: perhaps the reason an anonymous narrator works so well in *The Plague* is that Camus was anything but anonymous. By 1946, he was a national hero. He was entitled to speak for postwar values—both because of his status in the Resistance and because of his moral leadership as the editor in chief of *Combat*. Between the Liberation and 1947, when he left the newspaper, Camus published daily editorials on the state of France. His horror at the atomic bomb on Hiroshima, his editorials about the many divorces that followed the return of the prisoners of war to their families, his reports on Algeria, his critique of the purge of collaborators: all these positions made him a beacon of sanity for a nation in recovery. Now, within his fiction, Rieux's anonymity and desire to speak for an entire society gave Camus a way to be both historically specific and transhistorical. And in some ways this literary device was his revenge against a growing fame he had grown to hate, that separated him from his writing and reduced him to a last name. In 1946, he writes in his notebook: "What is a famous man? A man whose first name doesn't matter. For everyone else their first name has a particular meaning of its own."[8]

A parlor game: let's imagine that Camus wrote *The Plague* as an autofiction or a memoir based on his personal experience of occupied France, liberated France. It's not so easy to imagine the story Camus might have told. In 1964, the Camus specialist Germaine Brée wrote to Camus's widow, Francine, to try and get the details on his activities in the Resistance. Albert was not forthcoming about the Resistance period, Francine answered. He didn't like playing the old warrior. She tried to reconstruct the chronology, beginning with Camus's departure for France, his return to Oran, and then his relapse of tuberculosis, which sent him back to France for a mountain cure. He was in Le Panelier, a boarding house in the Massif Central, when the allies invaded North Africa and made travel to Algeria impossible for anyone in occupied France:

> He spent the winter of 1942–1943 in Le Panelier with trips to Lyon. It's probably in this period that he became friends with Leynaud, and I know that in Le Panelier he made contact with resistance groups.
>
> In late spring 1943 he settled in Paris where Gallimard offered him a job as reader. I suppose it was at that point that he began to work more closely with the underground newspaper *Combat*. . . .
>
> From this period, Albert told me about an episode where he was caught in a German roundup with the front page of the new issue of *Combat* in his pocket, and how he managed to destroy it in the courtyard where they'd been parked . . . and then the seizure of the collaboration newspapers and the publication of the new *Combat* during the first days of the Liberation of Paris. . . . His name at *Combat* was Bauchart. I found another false id card among his

papers in the name of Albert Mathé. Plus he received the medal of
the resistance. I'll send you a few pages that Jacqueline Bernard,
secretary of the *Combat* resistance movement, wrote for me (she
was arrested by the Gestapo in June 44, but had the good fortune
to return alive from Buchenwald).

That's all I can tell you for now. Jean Senart, who was also a
friend of Leynaud, told me he'd try to get other details.[9]

If Camus had written his war story as an autobiography, we
would have learned about the last months of the Occupation, about the arrest and deportation of Jacqueline Bernard
and her return. He would have written about the death by
firing squad of the poet René Leynaud, his close friend in
the *Combat* movement. Instead, in the novel, Camus's own
sorrow echoes in the senseless death of Tarrou. Tarrou with
the poet's gaze on the world, looking through the wrong end
of the binoculars. So many tragedies happened in occupied
France at the eleventh hour: reprisal massacres by the re-
treating SS in towns like Oradour-sur-Glâne, assassinations,
arrests, and deportations. Everything got worse before it got
better. And that was how Camus designed his fiction, with
the tragedy of Tarrou's death coming at the horrific turning
point of the pandemic. The narrator's closest friend and collaborator, someone to whom the reader is by now deeply at-
tached, dies just as the serum is beginning to save lives.

The disease finally retreats, and the city of Oran breaks
out in celebration. Dr. Rieux stands on the rooftop terrace
where he had once looked out at the city with his friend. Terraces are privileged places in Algeria, often connecting one
house to the next, serving as havens from the heat, zones
of sociability and respite from the day's labor. "It's as if the
plague never came up here," Rieux says. Now with Tarrou
gone, Rieux stands alone in that same spot, and the murmur

of the city below, lapping against the foot of the building like a wave, reminds him of the collective voice he's tried to channel throughout the novel.

In *The Rebel*, a book he considered a companion piece to *The Plague*, Camus delves further into the yearning that leads Rieux to say "we." Sometimes, he suggests, when we're overwhelmed by the strangeness of things, aware of our separateness from the universe, there comes an awakening, a consciousness that the plague is never ours alone. When Rieux looks out from the rooftop and feels the loss of his friend, he experiences a connection to a whole city whose losses and struggles he has chronicled: "here, high above all sorrow . . . Rieux felt himself join them."[10] The experience of a shared illness in the novel reappears in *The Rebel* as the preexisting condition for positive revolt. Camus, who loves a Nietzschean paradox, talks about saying no as the first step in creating change. Now, when I read the most famous line of *The Rebel*, I see Dr. Rieux's struggle against the annihilating force of the plague: "I rebel—therefore we exist."[11]

A collective voice isn't the same as an official one. On the radio, I listen to the rapidly changing stories from the French government. Cases of COVID have risen to the point where there are no more available beds in the hospitals, and the administration has designed "medicalized" train cars to transport ailing patients to regions outside Paris. I'm not allowed to leave France until I have a negative PCR test and a "certificate of recovery" from my doctor. My zones of trust and fear, too, are altered. I'm starting to think about perspective, to wonder what story the streets will tell.

These past few weeks, I've felt the first inklings of collective action, a growing awareness of injustice, a revolt against selfish individualism. How could we have had a Dr. Rieux narrating the epidemic in America when half the electorate barely admitted there was an epidemic? Whenever Donald Trump would acknowledge the disease, he represented the fight against COVID as a personal expression of toughness. To wear a mask was to admit weakness. The repression went beyond individual actions. COVID was an excuse for executive orders closing the borders of the nation against immigrants. In the Trump administration, every aspect of the disease was weaponized. Under Joe Biden, the ethics of care are yoked to economic recovery, to "shots in arms and money in pockets." Camus allegorized war as plague, but plague, too, can be deployed as a political allegory.

2 RAT EURYDICE

Laura

It's easy to take an animal for a sign. In the first pages of the novel, a plague-infected rat dies a cartoon death, pirouetting on the doctor's landing and collapsing in a heap. "From the dark end of the corridor, a large rat emerged with shaky steps and wet fur. The creature stopped," Camus writes, "seemed to try to catch its balance, started toward the doctor, stopped again, spun around with a little cry and finally fell, blood spurting from its parted jaws."[1]

Though it feels like high drama, Camus actually found this description of rat death in a medical source—the epidemiologist Adrien Proust's 1897 book *La défense de l'Europe contre la peste*. "Before the epidemic starts," Dr. Proust writes, "the animal comes out of its hole in the floorboards or in the ground below the house. It wobbles, spins around, spits blood, and perishes."[2] In mirroring this description, Camus places his rat in dialogue with previous plague accounts, and with the ways human knowledge about plague is preserved and transmitted. Using Dr. Proust as a source lets the rat represent the written history of the disease. Confronted by the mass die-off of rodents, Rieux's colleague Castel figures out the connection to plague by going to the library. "The rats died of the plague or something that very much resembles it," he concludes. "They put tens of thousands of fleas into circulation that will transmit the infection exponentially, if it isn't stopped in time."[3]

But instead of seeing that rat as the sign of an epidemic, Dr. Rieux looks at the animal and thinks of his wife, who is about to leave the city for a sanatorium in hopes of recovering from tuberculosis. "It wasn't the rat he was thinking of," Camus writes. "That spurt of blood reminded him of his own worry. His wife, who had been sick for a year, was supposed to leave the next day for a mountain retreat."[4] This projection on Dr. Rieux's part is a uniquely human pattern—we love to see the natural world around us through the lens of our feelings and relationships. Anthropomorphizing the animal's death (indeed, barely thinking of the rat itself) is a classic mistake: you think the natural world is a backdrop, a metaphor for human concerns, and yet you are already subsumed within it.

Dead rats are a sign of human plagues to come, but they are also carriers of plague memory, involuntary triggers of uneasiness in humans. For other citizens of the city, the revulsion and bewilderment the rats provoke read as a form of instinct, a primal response that something is amiss, a panic, even, at not being as separated as they might wish to be from the interconnected histories of other species. Though the humans in the novel think plagues are part of history, rather than daily life, they quickly discover that what happened in the world of Dr. Proust's book can happen to them. Adrien Proust, it turns out, was the father of the writer Marcel. Like his son's famous madeleine, the rodent troubles the veil that divides the now from the before. Dr. Proust's rat is a bridge between present and past, a sign that we are not invulnerable to the environmental experiences that have preceded us. It must have pleased Camus, who felt shut out by the literary opulence of Proust's milieu, to turn the Proustian tea-cake into a dead rat.

Then things get more complicated. As the epidemic crosses the species barrier and spreads to humans, it's no longer the rats who collapse for an audience as community transmission grows. The dramatic rat of the opening pages not only reminds the doctor of his wife—it also mirrors the opera singer who dies much later, at the height of the epidemic. In the middle of Christoph Gluck's opera *Orpheus and Eurydice*, which the trapped opera company has been performing over and over in quarantine, the singer playing Orpheus collapses at the crescendo of the piece, at the moment when he loses Eurydice, and the lovers become separated forever. As with the rat, the singer's internal struggle with illness can no longer be concealed—he comes out of the woodwork, dying in public and triggering horror. "He chose that moment to advance grotesquely toward the spotlight, spread his arms and legs in his costume from antiquity, and collapse in the middle of the pastoral elements of the stage set that had always been anachronistic, but that appeared so for the first time to the spectators, and in a horrifying way."[5] Here, the people have gone into the theater to try to escape the plague outside, and yet it has followed them. When the opera singer breaks character, the pastoral sets of antiquity suddenly lose their dramatic power and become the trappings of real death. The story of lovers separated by the grave isn't a myth anymore, but a very real anxiety. Orpheus, in this case, returns from the underworld like a plague rat—an opera singer whose beautiful voice may have infected the entire orchestra circle. He emerges into the living world, not as a bereaved husband, but as a vector of disease.

It fascinates me that Camus chose this particular opera to repeat throughout the plague. In the original story, the newlywed Eurydice gets bitten by a snake and dies. Orpheus makes a bargain with the gods to journey to the underworld and retrieve her, and she is allowed to return with him, as long as he never looks back at her on the way to the surface. But he loses his faith at the eleventh hour and turns around. The pact is broken, and the lovers are once again parted. The plot is all about a do-over—the chance to rectify the cruelty of an untimely death. Eurydice's death, the myth contends, was not supposed to happen when it did. Beautiful newly-weds are not supposed to drop dead. And one of the deepest human fantasies is that when something horrible and unfair happens, a force might intervene to allow another outcome. That the fact of death will be erased by the possibility of a second chance. The myth itself deflates this fantasy in the most painful way—when Eurydice calls his name, Orpheus can't help looking back at her, and she is forced to return to the underworld. "What should he do?" Virgil asks, "Whither should he betake himself having twice lost his wife?"[6] Orpheus kills himself (or else is brutally killed) in order to rejoin her. But Gluck's version of the myth is an odd one. In his opera, Orpheus gets not only a second chance but also a third. The god Amore takes pity on Orpheus and brings Eurydice back to life anyway, even though Orpheus fails to keep the bargain that will rescue her. The opera ends with a chorus of voices singing love's triumph. And yet, Gluck still called his opera a tragedy. As if to confirm that three brushes with death is a lot for any couple to survive.

Dr. Rieux, too, subscribes to the idea of a second chance. When he separates from his wife at the beginning of the novel, he says, "Everything will be better when you return. We'll start over." A few lines later: "He called his wife by her first name, and when she looked back, her face was covered with tears."[7] This moment is a role reversal—Rieux is an Orpheus who calls Eurydice's name, forcing her to look back. She is the one journeying to thwart untimely death, and it's Orpheus who can no longer follow her. Something breaks between them, and the foreshadowing image of the rat makes us suspect that it will never be repaired. In the next moment, the glass of the train windows comes between them, as if the gates of the underworld have already closed.

When the plague places the city in quarantine, everything outside it starts to resemble the afterlife. The dead pile up outside the city walls, forcing the officials to concede that "the accumulation of victims was, in fact, far greater than the possibilities offered by our little cemetery. No matter how many sections of the wall they knocked down, offering the dead a chance to escape into the surrounding areas, they quickly had to find another way."[8] The only people allowed to leave the city permanently are those who haven't survived.

As the dead roam the land outside Oran's walls, the sea, too, becomes a mythological space, a body of water in the underworld. When Tarrou and Rieux leave the plagued city to take a swim, they enter a deserted port where they are the only living humans. The guard at the gates doesn't want to let them through, but because they have their papers as health workers, they can go anywhere their jobs require, moving between the living and the dead. As Amore sings to Orpheus in Gluck's opera, "It is granted you to pass / the sluggish waters of Lethe alive!"

Shade-like and ghostly, the pale shadows of the moon greet Rieux and Tarrou in this strange gateway:

A moment later, the car stopped near the gates of the port. The moon had risen. A milky sky projected pale shadows everywhere.

The city ranged behind them and a hot, sick gust rose from it, pushing them toward the sea. They showed their papers to a guard who examined them for quite a long time. They passed through, and between the embankments topped with barrels, among the whiffs of wine and fish, they headed in the direction of the jetty.[9]

No longer a port for commerce, this place is still a portal where it's possible to depart into oblivion. But the form oblivion takes surprised me—in fact, I didn't notice it until I translated the swimming scene and saw, word by word, how much the sea resembles a rat:

It hissed softly at the foot of the big blocks of the jetty, and as they climbed them, it appeared, dense as velvet, supple and sleek as an animal. They sat on the rocks, turned toward the deep. The waters swelled and ebbed slowly. This calm breath of the sea made the oily glints on the water's surface emerge and disappear. Before them, the night was limitless.[10]

Remember the wet fur at the start of the novel? The fur of the dead rat whose blood makes Rieux think of his wife's tuberculosis? This vision of the sea as sleek, wet, oily fur offers a glimpse of these waters as a kind of origin point for the plague—a carrier of diseases that is nonetheless beautiful, otherworldly. The connection between blood and sea has a scientific basis, too, in that the human circulatory system is like a "private ocean."[11] Our plasma, the fluid that carries our blood cells, "has a concentration of salt and other ions that is remarkably similar to sea water."[12] Like blood, the ocean circulates disease, but also nutrients, oxygen. The sea reminds us of Rieux's wife through its breathing, something that Camus, as a tuberculosis patient, never took for granted. It's as if the sea has a kind of animalistic force, a rat-hiss that carries the memories of every plague that's come before, a limitless microbiome arriving and departing on the tide.

When they plunge into these oblivious waters, Rieux and Tarrou are temporarily liberated from their own particular plague: "For several minutes they moved forward with the same cadence and the same force, solitary, far from the world, freed at last from the city and the plague."[13] Neither one follows the other in or out of the water—instead, they swim at the same pace. There's no tragic moment here when one of them looks back and the other is consigned to death. That night, they are both allowed to return to life, and when they do, they find the disease has "forgotten them and this was good, and that now they must begin again."[14] But they don't have much time to enjoy the remaining days that have been granted to them.

Weeks later, when Tarrou dies of the plague, it's no coincidence that Camus describes his death as a drowning. The doctor is forced to watch as Tarrou, "this human form that had been so close to him," founders, "sinking before his eyes into the waters of the plague, and he could do nothing to stop the shipwreck. Once more, he had to remain on the strand, his hands empty and his heart twisted. . . ."[15] Tarrou returns from the underworld in the swimming scene, only to be dragged back into the rat-waters of the disease. As Camus says, the plague has a long memory—it "didn't forget anybody for long."[16]

Rieux gets to live, but he doesn't get any second chances at happiness. It's left to him to be the chronicler, the memory-worker. He remains on the shore of what happened so that he can pass on the knowledge and memory of the disease, and of people he lost. I feel for this Orpheus, stranded on the living side of ecological memory. And yet, his labor is necessary.

By representing plague in the ocean itself, Camus was ahead of his time. Just this year, an article was published in *Scientific American* by members of the Ocean Memory Project, a team of researchers who argue that "every aspect of this vast oceanic system can be viewed as holding memory, from short-term to long-term, individualized to collective."[17] For them, memories of SARS-CoV-2 exist in the microbial life of the ocean, where colonies of viruses and bacteria experience epidemics of their own. The "fluid interconnectivity" of our planet offers opportunities to acknowledge that we are inextricable from the vast underworlds of ecological memory. "As the novel coronavirus becomes more familiar to the human body," they write,

> it offers a memory of the deep connection that human evolution—all life—has to early ocean history. Might a shared focus on the surfacing of entrenched memories of human evolution, systemic racism and the trauma in individual lives lost galvanize humanity towards collective change that is mindful of our history and ecology?
>
> Is there a way for us to search—individually and collectively—for ways to shift the paradigm from "*ego to eco*"? From separated humans, fearful of each other and of nature, to an ecologically entangled sense of self? And what will be encountered on such a search? Pruned memories, lost archives, oceanic embedded histories that have largely escaped awareness? Like ocean memory itself, metaphor and scientific precision need not be in contradiction.[18]

If you've ever heard a rat hiss, it really does sound like the wavelets of a calm sea. In 2003, medical researchers in Algeria returned to Dr. Rieux's chronicle when eighteen cases of bubonic plague reappeared in Oran. Two patients fell into comas. As a result, Idir Bitam, a medical entomologist, led a team to collect fleas from rats in the surrounding areas. He was looking for traces of *Yersinia pestis*, the bacillus of the plague that, in Camus's words, "never dies or disappears." In the conclusion of his report, Bitam wrote:

> Rieux, the hero of Albert Camus' *La Peste*, aimed to relate the events of the plague outbreak in Oran in the 1940s with the highest objectivity. He stated that . . . plague can come back one day and he asked [us] to be aware when it did. Apparently plague has retired but is waiting in numerous foci and could reemerge. . . . The 'comeback' of plague in the region of Oran occurred in June 2003. In this study, we detected Y. pestis in rodent fleas collected from September 2004 to May 2005 in the same area as those plague cases occurred. Our results confirm that Y. pestis infection is still present in Algeria.[19]

Sometimes, what begins as literary allegory ends up as scientific fact. At least on this strange, watery world.

3 *LES SÉPARÉS*

Alice

At first, Camus wanted to call *The Plague* "Les séparés"—the separated ones. Separation was always Camus's own shadow theme, but for a long time all its twists and turns seemed remote to me.

I was in Paris when the city began its first official confinement, Tuesday, March 17, 2021, at noon. I set out at eleven to get a last walk in the Luxembourg Gardens, but it was too late; the park gates were already padlocked. Crossing the boulevard Raspail, I saw a florist carrying all his bouquets to the sidewalk. "Take them or they'll die," he said to no one in particular, "I'm closing in a few minutes." Passersby swooped down to grab their free flowers. They looked like panicked birds, pecking at the last blossoms. I remembered a story Roger Grenier had told me, about the men in his army unit in June 1940, standing at attention in a muddy field as their commanding officer announced the defeat of France. The men were crying and now so was I. Not weeping, but feeling the tears well up.

The night before, I'd watched the French president's speech, in which each new pronouncement began with the refrain "We're at war":

> We're at war. All actions of the government and the parliament
> must now turn toward the combat against the epidemic. Day and
> night, nothing must distract us.[1]

Camus created his plague allegory to turn the experience of
war into a disease. Now, in a reverse allegory, President Macron was making the experience of disease into a war. As
warriors, we would all need to download a form for permission to go to the pharmacy or the grocery store. The mar-
tial rhetoric didn't quite work. The French word *confinement*
(with its antonym *deconfinement*) is gentler than the American "lockdown," but it's still a separation from the world, an
isolation rather than a battle.

Separation is a slow, steady beat in *The Plague*, not only a
theme that Dr. Rieux will analyze in his plague chronicle but
a motor for the plot and a maker of images, present in the
smallest gestures of his characters. "And so each person had
to agree to live day by day," he writes, "facing the sky alone."[2]

Camus decides early on to foreground the way quarantine tears people apart. He experiments with a passage in
his notebooks, describing two kinds of separation that are
linked. The whole city is separated from the world, and the
people are separated from their loved ones: "And now probably it was not enough to be separated from the world itself, the plague still had to separate them from their modest
daily creations. After blinding their minds, it tore out their
hearts." Then he makes a practical decision about his book in
progress: "There are nothing but solitary men in the novel."[3]
In the end that wasn't strictly true, but for Camus, a world
with few women is a bleak place where romantic love is reduced to longing.

Separation, from the time he drafted the novel to its publication, was also the driving force of Camus's own experience. In November 1942, he was living in the mountainous

region of central France, near Lyon—the Massif Central. He had traveled there in August from Algeria for treatments for his tuberculosis, which had flared up badly after the publication of *The Stranger*. His wife, Francine, had come with him, but in early October she needed to return to Algeria for her teaching job. On November 8, the Allies invaded North Africa, and Algeria was cut off from mainland France for the rest of the war. Algeria became Allied territory, while France, which once had a so-called free zone, was now entirely occupied by the retaliating Nazis. There was no more free zone, no more travel, no more mail service between Allied North Africa and Nazified France. Camus had missed the last boat to Algeria. He couldn't even send a letter home.

Back in Oran, on New Year's Eve of 1942, Francine wrote to a friend in New York:

> This year's end finds me here with the Americans, while my husband is in France, unable to join me. I haven't had any news from him since November 11. We haven't had any luck. I believe Jeanne Terraccini told you that my husband had a relapse of his illness at the end of January. It was a low blow for him. But he has a great deal of courage. He went through another round of treatments and this summer we left for France so he could take a mountain cure. I left him in October to organize our life in Algiers for the winter (We had decided to move to Algiers). He was supposed to recuperate in France until the end of November. He was about to reserve a seat on the boat to come back when the Americans landed in Algeria. He would have been so happy to have been here.
>
> Clearly we were foolish. We wanted to act as if the war didn't exist. And the war has separated us.[4]

On November 11, the day Francine received her husband's last letter, he wrote in his notebook: "Trapped like rats."[5]

Separated, but also trapped. In *The Plague*, Camus reverses the geography of husband and wife: Dr. Rieux is trapped in Oran, and his wife leaves for the mainland, to take a cure in a sanatorium. She doesn't survive.

Dr. Rieux waits for his wife quietly, mournfully, as if he already senses she won't return. When the gates are closed, Rambert, a Parisian journalist who has come to Oran to file an investigative report on public health in the Arab neighborhoods, is trapped along with everyone else. He makes a deal with some shady characters on the waterfront to get out of the city. But at the last moment, in a dialogue carefully crafted by Camus, he decides to stay and joins the public health squads who are fighting the plague.

Rieux's separation from his wife at the train station at the start of the novel and Rambert's reunion with his partner at the end are bookends that express the strangeness of both separation and reunion. Camus didn't put much faith in perfect reunions. He wrote in *Combat*, in a June 1944 editorial: "Separation seems to me to be the rule and reunion only the exception."[6]

In *The Plague*, when Rieux bids farewell to his wife:

> He pressed her against him, and on the platform now, from the other side of the window, all he could see was her smile.
> "Please," he said, "take care of yourself."
> But she couldn't hear him.[7]

Dr. Rieux holds his wife in his arms, and in the space of a single sentence, he's on the other side of the train window, standing on the quai. Camus expresses Rieux's grief with the image of a glass barrier that always reminds me of the philosophical version of the same image in *The Myth of Sisyphus*: "A man is talking on the telephone behind a glass partition;

you can't hear him, but you see his incomprehensible dumb show; you wonder why he's alive."[8]

The separated lovers are silenced by the glass that comes between them like grief, while the man watching the pantomime in the phone booth doesn't feel much of anything except his own incomprehension. Both scenes take me back to the first months of the virus, to my separation from my friends, my students, and to the first courses I taught by Zoom. When you say goodbye to someone in the world, you get to watch them walk away, or get in a car, or weave through the security line in the airport until you can't see them anymore. In Zoom it's not quite sudden death. At the end of class, there's a brief second when the images of the students' faces freeze before disappearing in a flash. I want to run my index finger over the screen as if I could coax them back. Disbelief: we were talking, and then they were gone. By now, this way of parting has become familiar to me. Zoom loneliness, I call it, or in darker moments, Zoom death.

In Camus's novel, the problem of separation doesn't end with the end of the plague. When Rambert welcomes his true love at the same train station where Rieux said goodbye to his wife, he is crying too hard to know if the form he's embracing—"the form running towards him"—is still the person he knew.[9] There's a sense of danger in every reunion: Can the loved one be the same after a time of absence, or are all reunited lovers at risk of finding a stranger?

Camus didn't see Francine Camus for two years. But life went on. On D-Day, when Parisians were celebrating the allied landing in Normandy, Camus met the actress Maria Casarès. Their connection was immediate, intense. In October, his wife finally got a boat to mainland France to join her husband. Camus and Casarès separated.

On June 6, 1948, the exact anniversary, to the day, of their first meeting on D-Day, he and Maria Casarès crossed paths on the boulevard Saint-Germain. The filmmaker who makes this movie will have to decide where along that long street they meet: the Bac metro stop near Gallimard, the Café de Flore, the Odéon metro? Camus had just published *The Plague*, which was a runaway success. His twins were four years old. Maria had a new lover. I try to imagine them walking toward one another, the opposite of Orpheus and Eurydice, about to reunite for the rest of their lives.

In his December 1944 editorial in *Combat*, two months after Francine's return, Camus took stock of the situation. "Nostalgic longing, broken loves, ghostly dialogues carried on across the plains and mountains of Europe or sterile monologues conducted in the mind of one person awaiting reunion with another—such are the signs of these wretched times."[10] Again in spring, as the prisoners of war and deportees began to return to France, Camus remarked that the more private victory at war's end was the victory of the couple against separation. The sentiment reappears in his notebooks: "80% divorce among repatriated prisoners of war. 80% of human loves do not resist five years of separation."[11]

The ways and means of separation and communication during the current pandemic would have been inconceivable to anyone in Camus's generation, yet the deep processes he describes have helped me understand strange postmodern forms of separation mediated by technology. How many lovers have been separated, how many "ghostly dialogues" have been carried on across the globe on Zoom or FaceTime?

———

Rambert has always been my least favorite character in *The Plague*. Descending on Oran from out of town to get his story, he irritates Dr. Rieux with his questions, and Rieux questions him in turn: Will the newspaper give Rambert the freedom to totally condemn the terrible living conditions of native Arabs in Oran? The answer is no. So already I don't like him as a journalist. He isn't willing to risk the all-out condemnation, and his report on the lives of Arabs in the city will remain unfinished in the novel, swallowed up by his personal misery. I'm not touched by his love story, either, because I can't picture his lover in my mind. I don't know her name, or what she does. She's a cloud of his own regrets. Without much sympathy, I have to put up with his indulgent indecision, the should-I-stay-or should-I-go that became the pet question of so many privileged city dwellers during the first months of COVID, Parisians and New Yorkers with large country houses and gardens, people with options. A well-known French novelist made waves when she described her confinement in the countryside as a "fairy tale," an opportunity to write, to think, to revel in the beauty of nature. Readers were quick to point out that life in a two-hundred-square-foot garret in Paris with the walls pressing in, with no more job, was not a fairy tale.

In *The Plague*, beset by an impatience I can recognize in myself, Rambert starts to negotiate with the *passeurs*—the kind of people who, in Camus's world, might have escorted a Jewish family over the mountains to Spain. Cottard sets up the rendezvous at the shady restaurant in the Quartier Marine with Raoul and Garcia and Gonzales, Spanish gangsters in Oran, and they introduce him to their sailor friends. They mention a price of 10,000 francs, and there is a first meeting under the portico of the Cathedral, a second on the port in front of the monument to World War I dead. Camus takes his time describing this negotiation: there are false starts and people to meet and contacts lost, and then Rambert has to start all over again. He's doing it for love, he says, but he realizes that the quest itself has erased his companion: "he had somehow forgotten his wife by putting all his energies into searching for a gap in the walls that separated him from her." The trapped feelings of the plague overwhelm everything, even the person he's trying to reach. Paradoxically, the desire to unite with a lost love has become a kind of self-centeredness. But he excuses it by saying they hadn't been together for very long.

————

For a writer, the ultimate experience of separation is literary. How to take leave of a draft that isn't working, how to know that a book is finished and separate from the manuscript. Camus had trouble on both counts. From August 1942 to September 1943, he finished a first draft of *The Plague* that is almost unrecognizable.[12] The main character of this primitive version of *The Plague* is Philippe Stephan, a self-absorbed, suicidal classics teacher. Still troubled by his separation many years earlier from Jeanne, his unfaithful wife, he spends his time preparing a commentary on Thucydides and Lucretia and the Black Death of Athens. The work keeps him company during the plague. Some of Camus's notes indicate that Stephan will hang himself, others that he will live.

The sanatorium where he was treating his tuberculosis condemned him to monotony and to loneliness. The heating was terrible in his mountain lodging, and he was dreaming about going home and renting a villa in the heights of Algiers. But he was determined to make the best of it. In October 1942, Camus wrote to a friend, Lucette Maeurer: "At least I can continue to work here. I've gotten pretty far on *The Plague* but I think I need to start all over again."[13] When

Algeria was cut off from France in November, he knew for
sure that he would have to put his first version aside and
start again. Exile, separation, and solitude gave him the energy to conceive of a new draft, where the personal and the
political would come together in one collective experience
of plague. Stephan, with his existential dilemma over suicide and his dissatisfaction with love, must have started to
seem like a throwback to an earlier phase of Camus's thinking. Camus did away with him completely. Now, at the beginning of the novel, we meet Cottard, who has written in
chalk on his door "come in, I've hanged myself."[14] The gal-
lows humor sets the tone for the whole novel, tragic but also
funny. Grand, the civil servant who chooses his words carefully, cuts Cottard's noose down and saves him. Like his pre-
decessor Stephan, Grand is full of regrets for a long-ago wife
named Jeanne whom he didn't love well enough, and who left
him. Camus's own constant plans and readjustment of his
novel have their comic representative in the lovable Grand,
who can never get his sentence right: "One fine May morning, a svelte equestrienne rode a superb sorrel mare down
the flowering lanes of the Bois de Boulogne."[15] Grand, for all
his literary hesitations, turns out to be an effective fighter
of the plague through his work in the bureau of statistics.
Unlike most of the city government officials, he believes in
calling things by their names.

   We think that Camus stopped working on the first version of the novel in January 1943. He hadn't yet experienced
the death of his friend and fellow *Combat* member René Leynaud, shot by the Nazis for acts of resistance. He hadn't been
caught in a Nazi roundup and had to hide his copy of the
paper to save himself. Jacqueline Bernard, his coeditor at
Combat, hadn't yet been arrested and deported. He hadn't yet
waited for her to return. It's fashionable in literary criticism

to say that art is always disconnected from life. But in this case, at least, Camus's losses, the depth of his engagement and the risks he took, made their way into a very different version of his novel. He saves the true darkness of separation for the end, with the death of Rieux's wife. In the final version of *The Plague*, each character is painfully aware of their personal losses, of the absent loved ones who may or may not return.

Yet, in theory, the group effort of fighting the plague should have value surpassing the life of any one individual. But Camus doesn't come to that conclusion easily. The test case is Rambert, locked in his individual love story as surely as he's locked in the plague-ridden city. He's defensive about his choice not to join the public health squads. He confesses to Tarrou that he'd fought in the Spanish Civil War, where you were supposed to be heroic, ready to die for an idea. But no one in Oran is putting any pressure on him. Rieux points out that fighting the plague is not about an idea; it's about honesty, the frank confrontation of their situation. When Rambert learns from Tarrou that Rieux's wife is in a sanatorium in France, something clicks. It's a mysterious conversion, a sudden ability to withstand the grief of separation he shares with Rieux. He calls the doctor:

"Would you allow me to work with you until I find a way to leave the city?"

There was a silence on the end of the line, and then:

"Yes, Rambert. Thank you."[16]

4 ON RESTRAINT

Laura

The Plague was not an easy book to write. Camus was ill when he began it, then trapped by the borders keeping him in Nazi-occupied France. Apart from these difficulties, there was the pressure of authentically speaking up about the violence of World War II without falling into the nationalist heroics he deplored. Like most problems in art, the solution was to address it directly: in one of the most revelatory sections of the novel, the character Tarrou blurs the line between fancy rhetoric and violence. "I've heard so much reasoning that almost turned my head," he says, "and which had turned enough other heads to make them consent to killing, and I understood that all human sorrow came from not keeping language clear."[1]

All human sorrow! The boldness of this claim hints at how much Camus believed in words. *The Plague* is full of people who struggle to clarify their language and who strain to make it more precise—Grand, Rambert, Paneloux, and even Rieux all try (and sometimes fail) to express their deepest feelings through words. But unlike his characters, Camus managed to develop a style that could encapsulate feeling within the sentence structures themselves, a kind of syntax that could capture deep emotion in plain speech.

For example, the first time Rambert tries to get out of the city, the smugglers who might help him escape don't show up, and he despairs at the thought of having to retrace his steps:

> At that moment, in the night spanned by fugitive ambulances, he realized, as he would come to tell Doctor Rieux, that this whole time he had somehow forgotten his wife by putting all his energies into searching for a gap in the walls that separated him from her.[2]

Camus raises the emotional register of the language slightly here, but the words are quite plain, and most of the work is done by the structure of the sentence itself. Though the opening of the sentence promises immediacy, it is full of delays and distractions—the ambulances, the presence of the doctor, all the intervening time. The three prepositional phrases that front-load the sentence create the syntactic equivalent of the delayed gratification Rambert is experiencing. And the end of the sentence enacts the separation itself, forming a word-wall between him and his love, which in the French is even more difficult to surmount: *les murs qui le séparaient d'elle.*[3] The sentence ends with him and her and only "séparaient," the word for ongoing separation, divides them.

This stylistic strategy provoked a bizarre paradox. Critics have called (and continue to call) Camus's prose in *The Plague* "rigorously and studiously unbeautiful" or stoic or flat or even blank—and yet readers react to the prose with emotion, they find it powerful and sometimes tender.[4] I'd like, in this short essay, to explore the disjunction a little more—as a translator but also as someone who came to writing through poetry.

First, let me say that restraint is a tricky concept, a tangle of literary and emotional implications. It has been weaponized by conservative critics to argue for a kind of "appropriateness," to disavow the urgent necessity of radical self-expression. Restraint has also been mistaken for a kind of stiff-upper-lip style, a way of pushing feelings down (out of patriotism) so that horrific events (like wars) remain veiled from the public eye. Then there is restraint as a kind of humility before the unknown, the restraint of contemplating forces beyond a human scale. Late in life, Jacques Derrida, who also grew up in Algiers, linked restraint to the hush of faith, "scruple, hesitation, indecision, reticence (hence modesty, respect, *restraint* before that which should remain sacred, holy, or safe: unscathed, immune)."[5] Camus's character Tarrou, who wants to be a secular saint, isn't so far from Derrida's idea. For Tarrou, clarity in language prevents loss of life, and restraint is a kind of earthly religion, a path of "clear speech and action."[6]

As a secular person and as a person who felt compelled to bear witness, Camus had to develop an idea of restraint that was compatible with confronting harsh truths. But he was also troubled by the rarity of restraint in the aftermath of World War II—a lack of clemency, a quickness to defer to the binaries of good and evil, us and them. These forms of Manichean thought proved that simplicity in language could also lead to extremism. In 1948, the same year *The Plague* came out in English translation, Camus published "Letters to a German Friend," where he explicitly addressed the problems with these binaries. "When expressed forcefully," he wrote, "truth wins out over falsehood. . . . We are fighting for fine distinctions, but the kind of distinctions that are as important as humanity itself. We are fighting for the distinction between sacrifice and mysticism, between energy and violence, between strength and cruelty, for that even finer distinction between the true and the false."[7] Unlike falsehoods, truth, for Camus, requires a certain delicacy of expression, the fine distinction between clarity and simplicity. The syntax of this passage parodies the structure of binary thinking, but the words themselves counteract simple opposition. In fact, each pair is designed to provoke questions—where does sacrifice bleed into mysticism? How could there be a fine distinction between the true and the false? To get at some sense of authenticity, reality, truth, Camus used syntax that is clear but not reductive. In "Letters to a German Friend" and in his speech "The Human Crisis," he hoped for a community of individuals who could disarm hatreds and stereotypes, but he knew that such a world could only be possible if humans acknowledged their capacity to carry the venom of extremist thinking, and to turn people's heads with its rhetoric.

Plenty of venom, conscious or unconscious, can emerge through the flourishes of style. As W. G. Sebald points out, writers who attempt to bear witness to horrific events can fall prey to their own technique. His book *On the Natural History of Destruction* explores the few texts that attempt to describe the firebombing of Germany during World War II and the civilian casualties that resulted. In one essay, Sebald quotes the writer Arno Schmidt for his excesses of metaphor, excesses that lead Schmidt to describe the smoke after an air raid as a woman: "a fat-lady cloud stood up above the warehouse, puffed out her round belly, and belched a pastry head high into the air." The depiction of this cloud-woman is both sexist and not particularly moving. It's possible, here, for a reader to forget the loss of life this cloud signifies. As a response, Sebald writes that "the author certainly intended to conjure up a striking image of the eddying whirlpool of destruction with his exaggerated language,

but I for one, reading a passage like the following, do not vi-
sualize the supposed subject: life at the terrible moment of
its disintegration. . . . I do not see what is being described;
all I see is the author, eager and persistent, intent on his lin-
guistic fretwork."[8] The author is too visible here, and in his
eagerness to convey the intensity of destruction, he robs it
of all power—the style serves as a screen between author
and reader so that the horror of what's being represented is
blunted into a kind of literary fancy.

By contrast, *The Plague* uses few instances of figurative
language and, at the sentence level, rarely extends a metaphor. This aspect of the book has, at times, confused its readers, not to mention its translators. In the case of Stuart Gilbert, who lived through World War II and translated the book
in the immediate postwar period, the novel's plainer moments seem to provoke anxiety—he meddles with them to
make them closer to heroic postwar rhetoric. Where Camus
writes "they must begin again" (*il fallait recommencer*), Gilbert adds a mythological flourish: "they must set their shoulders to the wheel again."[9] These inner workings of restraint
are counterintuitive—often the less drastically the writer expresses an emotion, the more forcefully a reader can feel it.
Naming a feeling or conjuring it through elaborate flourishes
can be deflating, reductive. Camus's lack of stylistic padding
enables him to make his work harrowing. In a moment of the
novel that has been read by critics as Camus's acknowledg-
ment of the Nazi death camps, he writes, "And since a dead
man carries no weight unless you've seen him dead, a hundred million corpses strewn across history are nothing but
smoke in the imagination" (*une fumée dans l'imagination*).[10]
Robin Buss, who translated the novel in 2001, blinks here,
using "a mist drifting through the imagination."[11] By turning smoke into drifting mists of memory, Buss represents

the veil humans place between themselves and the dead, rather than what's left of the bodies. Instead of obfuscating, Camus's original metaphor tricks us into looking at what we don't want to see.

Confronted with the horror of death and ruin, Sebald identifies "the moral imperative for at least *one* writer to describe what happened in Hamburg on that night in July." When Sebald praises the writer Hans Erich Nossack, it's for his directness: "The tone here is that of a messenger in classical tragedy." As Alice points out in her essay on the narrator of *The Plague*, Dr. Rieux has some of this directness. He is a messenger, the counterpoint to Camus's narrator in *The Stranger*. Where Rieux is a "we," Meursault is a hollow "I"; he lacks a sense of community. The endings of the two novels represent two forms of immersion in the world. Or perhaps two ways in which the world absorbs human emotion. Where Meursault is a loner, someone who decides to open himself "to the tender indifference of the world,"[12] Rieux is a community member whose task is "to write simply" what the indifference of the world has thrown at him.

Of course, Camus was also trying to create an allegory, and in that sense, Rieux's task was always simpler than Camus's. Yet in this pandemic year, *The Plague* has been tested as a direct chronicle of illness and held its own. We have all, to some extent, become residents within its chapters. Many of the novel's details feel more realistic than your average allegorical gesture—the mastic trees, the skies, the understandable hypochondria, the heartlessness of bureaucracy, the emptiness of the shelves. In the midst of all this, I've had to restrain myself from bringing my reading experience onto the page. It would've been so easy to use the words in the news, to choose "vaccine" instead of "serum," to put my own frustrations in Rambert's mouth, or worse, Rieux's, to make

the prefect of Oran sound a little too much like Trump. I felt
this mirroring all year as I translated the novel in quarantine, as if the events of the world might become legible, rising through the ink shadow that signals the following page.

Perhaps *The Plague* holds up so well as a chronicle of
real illness because more than some of his contemporaries, Camus had an intense and highly specific relationship
with the natural world. Though he was criticized by Roland
Barthes and Jean-Paul Sartre for representing the Nazi Occupation through a biological phenomenon, there is a certain humility to this choice, a certain refusal to put human
intervention on a pedestal. "There are two sorts of efficac-
ity," Camus writes in *The Rebel*, "that of typhoons and that of
sap."[13] As Sebald proves, there is a great deal of restraint in
the reality of natural history, in trying to describe the world
plainly and precisely, but without oversimplification. This
use of description presents another paradox of restraint,
that the world itself is dramatic enough—if you look at it
closely, these images can express intensity without much
embellishment. Channeling emotion through observation
can be another way to express a feeling without naming it.

Here, I'm reminded of the first rat Dr. Rieux observes on
his landing, and the way it makes him think of his wife's illness. By describing how the animal collapses and coughs
blood, he accesses both the pain of his wife's symptoms
and the fact that they are ever-present in his mind. In a re-
strained way, what the doctor notices lets us understand the
true danger of his wife's condition without having to say it
directly. Restraint is sometimes the act of watching what dis-
turbs another's eye.

The craft of observation, of image making, is closely related to poetry. Though *The Plague* combines Camus's stylistic facility with fiction, with philosophical essay, and with

the dialogue of a play, there was another, less obvious genre that also influenced him—his early lyric essays, the writing that is closest to a kind of poetry about the natural world. In Ellen Conroy Kennedy's brilliant translations, "Nuptials at Tipasa" opens like this:

> In the spring, Tipasa is inhabited by gods and the gods speak in the sun and the scent of absinthe leaves, in the silver armor of the sea, in the raw blue sky, the flower-covered ruins, and the great bubbles of light among the heaps of stone. At certain hours of the day the countryside is black with sunlight. The eyes try in vain to perceive anything but drops of light and colors trembling on the lashes. The thick scent of aromatic plants tears at the throat and suffocates in the vast heat.[14]

Today, this would be called a prose poem—Camus's early voice at its wildest. And yet, there is a kind of restraint here, too, in delaying the self to foreground the landscape. Here, the "I" is withheld until the end of the paragraph. He begins with the lyric voice as an *eye* rather than an "I," a lens through which a reader is guided to observe the world. The intensity of this language serves to plunge us into the scene, to make us feel the granular detail of the sunlight, the rocks, the smell of the foliage. By immersing himself in the world, by placing suffocation in the heat and the scent of absinthe rather than in his own lungs, Camus withholds his actual situation—as someone who had tuberculosis, his own struggles with illness made him confront his own mortality. There is a sincere urgency in this beauty—you can only be so arrogant when you know you're going to die, when your body is already fighting for survival. These essays prove that restraint isn't the same thing as moderation—restraint can't exist without deep feeling on the part of the writer, without

intensity to harness. These early pieces read like the mani-
festos of someone trying to merge with a landscape as a way
out of himself. This kind of "style incarnate" is, for Camus,
what gives the written word power. To return to *The Rebel*:
"Through style, the creative effort reconstructs the world,
and always with the same slight distortion that is the mark
of both art and protest. . . . Art is an impossible demand
given expression and form."[15] Remember what I've seen. Feel
something of what I feel.

More than any other literary experience, translating
Camus has taught me that restraint isn't for the writer; it's
for the reader. By holding back the dazzle for a moment, a
writer can let someone look directly through the page, at the
part of the world that hurts.

5 FIELDWORK

Alice

The month war was declared, Camus wrote down a conversation he had with his mother. In his novel, he reproduces the dialogue, but he changes the word "war" to "plague":

> "Are they going to keep the lights scarce for the length of the plague?" asked Mme Rieux.
> "Probably."
> "Just as long as this doesn't last until winter. It would be sad, then."
> "Yes," said Rieux.[1]

In Mme Rieux, Camus borrowed many traits from his own mother, Catherine Sintès Camus, who lived in poverty, never learning to read or write. She was partially deaf and almost never spoke. She also had a limited vocabulary, managing to support her family by cleaning houses.[2] In *The Plague*, the love between mother and son takes place without words: "He and his mother would always love each other in silence. And she would die in turn—or he would—without them ever, during their whole lives, being able to get any closer to admitting their tenderness."[3] She was always an enigma to her son.

Tarrou, in his notebooks, gives the fullest portrait of Dr. Rieux's mother. He discerns a powerful gleam in her, a mysterious light whose goodness he recognizes but whose source he can't quite place:

> Tarrou particularly concentrates on the way Mme Rieux withdrew; the way she had of expressing everything in simple sentences; on the particular preference she had for a certain window, opening onto a quiet street, and where she sat up, quite straight, in the evenings, with calm hands and an attentive gaze until dusk had filled the room, making her into a black shadow in the gray light that darkened little by little before dissolving her motionless silhouette; on the lightness with which she moved from room to room; on the goodness she had never exactly shown in front of Tarrou, but whose gleam he recognized in all she did and said; last, on the fact that, according to him, she knew everything without ever pondering it, and that with so much silence and shadow, she could keep up with any sort of light, even if it was the light of the plague.[4]

Camus has created a transfiguring metaphor: Mme Rieux's power is her shadow. She's able to absorb the disease, extinguish its glare with her gentle strength. After Tarrou contracts plague, she convinces her son to ignore the rules that would send him to the isolation wards. Instead, she asks to keep Tarrou with them, so she can tend to him during his night of suffering, never faltering in her quiet vigil. She isn't afraid, nor does she tire. Tarrou's last energy is spent gazing at her intensely, as if he might finally glean her secret—or as if she had the key to release him from his struggle. From her armchair, Mme Rieux puts a finger to her lips to calm him, stands by his bedside, straightening his bolster and placing her hand on his damp, feverish head. The last muffled sounds Tarrou makes are to thank her. When Bernard Rieux returns, his friend gradually sinks "into the waters of the plague."

———————

Catherine Sintès Camus is buried in the Bru Cemetery in Algiers down the street from the Maquam Echahid, the monument to the martyrs of the revolution. Everyone knows the monument, but today few people visit the European cemetery. Even more silent than a regular cemetery, it looks out over the bay, a series of terraces so steep you have the feeling that a gust of wind might send all the tombstones tumbling down the hillside toward the cargo ships in the port below. In the upper ranges are the tombs of the great European Moudjahidine, the French who fought for the revolution and chose Algerian citizenship: Pierre and Claudine Chaulet are there, and Evelyne Safir, their graves scattered with dried flower wreaths. Catherine Sintès Camus's grave is below, in the very last row of the terrace, along the cemetery's lower boundary. I pay her a visit every time I'm in Algeria. On one of these trips, I noticed that her row of tombstones had been invaded by sprouting ailanthus, tree of heaven. In reality, it's neither tree nor bush nor weed, but all three at once. The plant is a familiar sight with its skinny leaves and stubborn trunks, always happy to grow between stones and broken concrete, thriving in landfills and empty lots and along abandoned train tracks, loving anywhere the soil has been disturbed. Ailanthus is an invasive species, killing and crowding out native plants. A tree loaded with the symbolism of invasion was making itself at home in the European cemetery.

To reach the last row of tombstones, my companions,

Père Guillaume Michel and Djamel Hachi, and I had to wade through the stuff, flattening it with our heels. It's also called "a stink tree," I discovered, because it really does smell very bad. The only viable competitors for the stink trees were thorny bushes that cut into my bare ankles. When we arrived at Catherine Camus's simple grave, we saw that a piece had broken off the bottom of the tombstone. Was it damage from a storm? It didn't look deliberate. We took careful measurements, thinking that we'd hire a stone mason to restore it, either by replacing the whole slab or reattaching the broken piece with cement and retracing the engraved letters, which had begun to fade.

We could still make out the names of two other members of the family. Anthelmette Bron, listed as "Widow Bouchut," who died February 2, 1946, and François Yvars, who died July 30, 1953. From what I've been able to learn, François Yvars was the son of Catherine's sister Marguerite, who'd married Michel Yvars. Camus gave the name Yvars to the main character in his story "The Silent Ones" about workers in a barrel shop who wage a silent strike. The widow Bouchut is more obscure. The Algiers daily *L'écho d'Alger* printed an obituary in 1938 for Philibert Bouchut, a butcher. Condolences were associated with the Acault family. Gustave Acault, fifteen years younger than Philibert Bouchut, was a surrogate father to Camus, and he, too, was a butcher. I wondered if he might have been Bouchut's nephew. In any case, we were looking at a family crypt of sorts, though modest in the extreme.

Djamel and I stopped chatting about the inscriptions on the tomb so that Père Guillaume could say a prayer. He pointed out that we represented the three branches of monotheism, Catholicism, Judaism, Islam. The prayer was very simple, about honoring and protecting the grave and the memory of Catherine Camus.

We hiked up the hill. Halfway, we passed a small house, where a guardian was living amidst the European graves, enjoying the rare quiet within the city. Finally, we entered the lodge at the entry to the cemetery where the registers are kept. We were greeted by a small, wiry man who looked about fifty. With his help, we studied register after register, tracing the purchase history of the plot. In September 1960, the month Catherine Camus died, Gustave Acault's widow, Marie, her next of kin, renewed a plot originally purchased fourteen years earlier for Anthelmette Bron. That fourteen-year concession had lasted through the death of François Yvars in 1953. Fifteen years, we learned, is the minimum duration for a plot in this cemetery. Grave sites could also be bought for thirty-year terms or in perpetuity. Catherine Camus died only nine months after her famous son perished in a car crash on the highway between Sens and Paris. That September, Algeria was two years from independence. Marie Acault did not choose perpetuity.

I told the guardian that I hoped they could clear out the mess of weeds around the grave and that we in turn would have the tombstone repaired by a stonemason. There are elaborate agreements between France and Algeria where European graves are concerned, and this cemetery, like the Bologhine Cemetery in the old Saint-Eugène neighborhood, is carefully tended. The guardian said it was fine for us to hire an independent mason. If we came back the next morning at 8:00 a.m., we could show his ground crew the spot, and they'd go after the brush.

6 HALF-LIFE

Laura

By the roadside, a small dirt driveway creates the illusion of a respectful distance between the living and the dead. Cars speed by as we pull onto the shoulder between the freshwater spring and the bluff where dry hills fall away into the sea. Two giant mastic trees hover over the wall like clouds, their dense, fragrant leaves obscuring the branches. Tombstones lean out of the shadows, cracked teeth in the yawn of a sunken grave. The place is beyond abandoned—no one can tell us who holds the lost keys to these gates.

This is Oran's Cimetière des Cholériques, a colonial cemetery that got its name from an 1849 cholera epidemic that was so bad it crowded this graveyard until there was no space left. Locals say that only the rich had headstones here. The poor who died in the epidemic were buried in mass graves like the ones Camus describes in *The Plague*, pits dug from "a bare space covered with mastic trees."[1] The Cimetière des Cholériques is barely noticeable from the road, eclipsed in the memory of French settlers by the Cimetière Chrétien that succeeded it up on the plateau.

In the landscape of independent Algeria, the half-life of colonization is in that cemetery, where the French government still pays to maintain the graves.[2]

Though the Cimetière Chrétien was the one used by the settler colonial population of Oran during Camus's time, these earlier graves along the ravine were the burial grounds that drew his imagination, both in *The Plague* and in his essay "The Minotaur, or Stopping in Oran." These older cemeteries are, by his reckoning, a testament to a harsh beauty that becomes hospitable only in death. The pared-down lyricism of his essay hides a great deal of human misery—in fact, despite a direct comparison with the "gentleness" of the cemeteries of Algiers in the previous sentence, Camus seems to forget that he is talking about a human resting place: "In Oran," he writes, "above the Ras-El-Aïn ravine, facing the sea for once, laid out against the blue sky are fields of chalky, crumbly pebbles set blindingly on fire by the sun. In the midst of these dead bones of the earth, here and there a crimson geranium lends its life and fresh blood to the landscape. The whole town is held fast in a stone vise."[3] Rather than the remains of people, we have fossils, the "dead bones of the earth." Looking down over colonial-era Oran, Camus describes the buildings as "scattered, brightly colored cubes," and the trees in the business district as a "petrified forest." In these dry heights of Oran's necropolis, Camus's view of the city is almost posthuman, or at least, posthuman memory. And his sense of time is geological, the timescale of fossilization, erosion, subsidence, climate. In his essay, the graves have been reduced to elements of landscape: sun, stones, sky, and petals of blood. Yet the historical forces that brought these dead to this place have not been forgotten.

Oran was founded by Andalusian Muslim traders in the tenth century, when a walled city was built around a casbah.

The name is first cited in 977 by the Arab geographer and writer Ibn Hawqal.[4] His book *The Face of the Earth* describes Oran this way: "Ouahran is such a safe harbor and so sheltered against all the winds that I don't believe it has an equal in all the Berber lands. . . . The settlement is surrounded by a wall and irrigated by a stream that comes from outside; the edges of the valley where this stream flows are crowned with gardens bearing all sorts of fruit."[5] Many attempted to occupy this Berber and Arab trading settlement, and over its history, the city had temporary roles as a colony for Moors fleeing Christianity, a pirate enclave, a Spanish conquest, an Ottoman base, an earthquake disaster, a community for Turkish Jews, and a French colonial port. It's now the second-largest city in Algeria.

For much of its early history, the invading forces who controlled Oran were under siege from the native Oranians and their allies who wanted to liberate their city. As a place with both a natural port and a spring, the location was strategic, and the "stone vise" of Oran was a highly defended fortress in a battle plain. Miguel de Cervantes, who visited Oran, even wrote a play about the 1563 siege, when Hasan Pasha came with an army from Algiers to retake the city from the Spanish.[6] Between 1509, when it was taken from the Berber kingdom of Tlemcen by the Spanish, and 1962, when it became independent from French colonial rule, outside forces attempted to control Oran and surveil its native inhabitants. Under French rule, the city was segregated, and the native population was displaced violently and ghettoized in a district outside the city walls called the Village Nègre.[7] During the French settler-colonial period, Oran housed a greater percentage of Europeans than any other city in North Africa. Significantly for *The Plague* and Camus's World War II allegory of Paris under the Nazis, colonial Oran was an occupied city.

If disease and war can ride the same two-way street of metaphor, then the city of Oran has seen its share of outbreaks. Epidemics of cholera, bubonic plague, typhus; invading armies, settler-occupation, and autocratic rule. Before it was the Cimetière des Cholériques, it was the Cimetière Espagnol, or the Cimetière Ras-El-Aïn. These violent changes created erasures, omissions, and revisions in the historical record—visible in the piles of old maps. In our current moment, the layers of remembering and renaming have moved online, where a chaotic proliferation of blogs and Facebook pages are devoted to old postcards and photos from the French colonial era. These sites, with names like *Nostalgérie* and *Alger à une certaine époque*, are problematic spaces, where *pieds-noirs* post their memories of segregated neighborhoods. Underneath almost every post, a dedicated commenter named Imad Daas has written "Époque merdique de la colonisation."[8]

During Camus's time, the French settlers still tried their best to erase Oran's past, keeping the native population segregated behind the army barracks, renaming streets, installing monuments, building a new cemetery. For Camus, the resulting majority-European neighborhoods of Oran had few signs of life besides making money. Here the Oranians are the colonizers, those who live in the French parts of the city. He writes in "The Minotaur":

> But except for the Spanish district, you find a city with its back to the sea, built turning in upon itself, like a snail. Oran is a long circular yellow wall, topped by a hard sky. At first, one wanders around the labyrinth, looking for the sea as for Ariadne's sign. But one turns around and around in the stifling yellow streets. In the end, the Oranians are devoured by the Minotaur of boredom. The Oranians have long since stopped wandering. They have let the monster eat them.[9]

Considering the history of Oran, "boredom" is an odd word. In a way, it's a false boredom, the illusion of colonial ennui that masks the injustice the French created. It's the boredom of a repressive space where everyone who isn't European has been violently excluded. The opposite of wandering is stopping, and even in this early essay, the French part of the city has a kind of colonial rot, a fortification alienated from the sea, its primary means of departure. Even before he writes *The Plague*, Camus describes Oran like a city in quarantine, trapped between its walls and its sky. Access to the harbor was geared toward trade and control, not human pleasure. In fact, before the French built a walkway along the bluff overlooking the port, they established pipes to carry wine from the vintners down to the docks to be collected in casks and exported. While the colonial lifeblood of Algerian wine flowed invisibly to the ships, and the wealthy Europeans enriched themselves with this vampirism, the city lay still, stifling in its heat. Some of Oran's strangest features remained out of sight, underground.

After the Spanish took the city in the sixteenth century, they built a network of forts surrounding the Ras-El-Aïn ravine, to keep a lookout from the heights where the plateau dips down to a spring that provided water for the city. The original location of the cholera cemetery was outside the walls of the Spanish fort called San-Fernando, which was destroyed when the Ottomans took Oran in 1708. The fort was turned into living space, but its subterranean defenses remained—beneath the fort, a network of tunnels connected it to other forts and secret exits where those trying to hold the city could create explosions to surprise an attacking army. Some of the subterranean tunnels had no exits and were so dense and complex that even the Spanish engineers who had built them referred to this network as "el laberinto," the labyrinth.[10]

Did Camus know that the plague cemetery was built above a labyrinth? That a vast and complex network of tunnels was branching under the graves? Were these graves under the mastic trees dug, or did the early French settlers simply bury their dead in the underground vaults of previous occupiers? Without access to the cemetery, it's hard to know. But it would be like Camus to base his mythological minotaur on a concrete feature of Oran's subterranean landscape. His essay is an invitation to wonder—what tribute could be paid to the minotaur at the center of these layered ruins entrapping the city in a maze?

But let me not get lost in it. As Camus was aware, myth and allegory share a common danger in that they create a narrative template, a way to read similarities into events whose specific horrors threaten to be relativized by comparison. Roland Barthes raised just such an objection to *The Plague* when it was published, criticizing Camus for transposing a Nazi force into an outbreak of disease. To me, as I translate Camus at the end of a long year of plague and a series of autocratic attempts by Donald Trump to hijack the democratic process, Camus's response to Barthes continues to resonate. "Terror has many faces," he replied, "which justifies that I named none of them in order to strike at them all."[11] In seeking a pretext to write about war, Camus gave us a narrative of community trauma and resistance that still has the capacity to teach us. The resonance of *The Plague* during the COVID-19 epidemic might well be due to the fact that the book is about both overcoming disease *and* resisting fascist ideology. The scholar Debarati Sanyal puts it well when she uses Camus's comment about the novel to describe the narrative patterns in his work, how they remain applicable to contemporary injustices. "I suggest instead that these allegories teach us how to read multiple histories at the same time," she writes, "to glimpse familiar features across the many faces of terror without petrifying them into a timeless mask of catastrophe."[12]

Without the glimpse Camus offers of those familiar features, and their resonances with our present moment, we might not have needed a new translation. And I would never have stood by the side of the road in Oran, looking for a cholera cemetery shaded by mastic trees, for the sense of abandon he captured in his writing. This roadside memory is part of translation craft—I was trying to layer my own sight of these graves with Camus's, to travel the labyrinthine paths of his associations. But the living city felt divided from the landmarks of illness in the book. In the streets crowded with commuters and vendors, we'd laughed when we saw a lone dead rat in the gutter. Our friend Sarah asked if I wanted to take a picture "for research."

Later, we drove back down the cliff road, along Oran's old tramway route. In *The Plague*, these trams are repurposed to carry the dead who have been killed by the plague. In one of the most beautiful passages in the novel, Camus describes the illicit ceremony for these victims:

> You could see, in the heart of each night, all along the cliff road, strange convoys of trams without passengers, wobbling above the sea. The city residents finally figured out what was happening. And despite the patrols that forbade access to the cliff road, groups often managed to slip in among the rocks that overhung the waves, to throw flowers onto the trolley cars as they passed. Then you could hear the trolleys jolting on through the summer night, with their cargo of flowers and the dead.[13]

Here the living sneak between the rocks and emerge to surprise the dead, not with explosions from the labyrinth, but with the flowers of a forbidden memorial.

A month after I returned from Oran, a COVID quarantine trapped fifty million people in Hubei province. Now when I read these passages from the novel, I see the line of army trucks in Bergamo, the fresh graves dug on Hart Island, the expansion of cemetery walls. Research, accuracy, connotation—these are all things I recognize, but I no longer know what place the elements of translation hold. I'm no longer just a translator getting closer to her subject, a researcher cultivating memory, observing an epidemic from the safe distance of history. I live in the world of this book. Now I understand I always did.

7 ATMOSPHERIC CHANGES

Laura

I. PLAGUE SPRING

The city I live in is still sometimes called "the city of no illusions." Except for walks with the dog, I haven't left the house in weeks. Time is sluggish in Buffalo, but the daffodil buds have begun to fatten, compelled by the passing days. It's the start of our first quarantine spring, and every week the words pile up. The deadline for my translation is approaching. April brings life and fiction into lockstep—in upstate New York, and in the plague novel on my desk, spring is just the start of the story, rising with a certain panic.

"Fat clouds ran from one horizon to the other," Camus wrote, "covering the houses with shadows that gave way, after they passed, to the cold, golden light."[1] In *The Plague*, the sky is a protagonist, as are the walls, and the people are caught in a tug-of-war between them, a sinister alternation of endlessness and barriers. As the character Tarrou says, they are trapped "between the sky and the walls of their city."[2] Walking in my own streets, I've noticed that people's moods do change according to the weather—for the first time, neighbors are standing on street corners, looking up at the clouds. Yesterday, I crossed the street to avoid the shadow side. Then I noticed almost all the other pedestrians had done the same, moving up the block, six feet apart, under the same city-sized bubble of sky.

Because the park is crowded, I go to the cemetery, and several people I know have started to do the same. It's strange to occasionally run into a friend among the aisles of graves, as if this were a normal place to wander, like a supermarket or a busy street. In the midst of the pandemic, the paths of the dead have been reintroduced into the rest of the city's green space. This is the one place in Buffalo where there are no sirens, where everyone is already out of danger. There are blooming trees in the cemetery, and deer with a genetic mutation that turns their fur white. But I come here just to watch the drama of movement—the cloud shadows sliding over the glistening fields.

These are vast sweeps, warm fronts covering hundreds of miles, but they are also predictable, an oracle of bright green pixels on the radar screen. I've always liked to check the weather in moments of uncertainty. As the weeks of isolation pass, I find my taste for speculation is gone. The unknowns of the coming months have worn it out. I'd like to remember the grass blades, the slow spring sunshine, the two almonds of a deer hoof, pressed in the mud of the stream. I've missed so much; I don't want to lose the raw clarity that grief sometimes lends to the world. Standing among the trees, with their neon clusters of newborn pollen, I worry that if I don't *choose* how to remember this time; then this pandemic will become something subliminal, suppressed into my muscles, encoded into my body like a habit.

But do we really get to choose what we remember—or only what we write down? In *The Plague*, the narrator Rieux includes a description of the weather in almost every section of his chronicle. He marks time with the sky like some kind of mariner, sailing across a swath of minutes, notching hours in a cloud clock whose hands are the winds and the sun. And in one sense, he was following tradition. Many early plague chroniclers also noted the weather, since winds and vapors were believed to be vectors of disease. The record of Oran's devastating 1849 cholera epidemic was no exception. "The atmosphere was broiling all summer long" begins the arch-priest of Oran's cathedral in his account, "Le choléra":

> Thick mists, passing almost constantly, had made the tempera-
> ture even more trying, and despite the lateness of the season, they
> still persisted; the air was drenched with humidity, and a truly tor-
> rid heat was sapping energies, softening courage, irritating minds,
> pushing everyone toward imprudence, making way for a terrible
> scourge.[3]

This "unhealthy humidity" makes the doctors of the town despair of being delivered from the epidemic. As the arch-priest's chronicle shows, meteorology in a plague narrative is not just description—it's also a source of suspense, since the whims of the skies were thought to influence the progress of disease. In several of the nineteenth-century medical sources Camus consulted as he researched his novel, humidity was cited as a factor that propagated the plague bacillus, as was "miasma" or "bad air." We now know that the relationship between climate and plague transmission is complex and sometimes contradictory, but in the 1800s, popular opinion followed a terrifyingly simple trajectory: miasma, disease, death.

For Camus, opening *The Plague* in spring creates drama as the rising heat and humidity bring the potential for illness. The season is beautiful and ominous. On the same day that Dr. Rieux discovers that the reserves of plague serum are exhausted, he reports that "from all the surrounding areas, spring had arrived at the markets. Thousands of roses fanned out in vendors' baskets along the sidewalks, and their sugary smell floated throughout the city." The air is not just atmospheric here, it's also deeply dissonant. Like the plague doctors who filled their beaked masks with flowers, the roses at the market are masking the rise of something more sinister. Rieux watches the sky because he's afraid the rising heat will make people sicker. Soon everyone else is watching the weather, too. On one of the first hot days in the novel, the connection between plague and weather becomes part of the public perception:

> The colors of the sky and the smells of the earth that made up the passage of the seasons were, for the first time, meaningful to everyone. Everyone understood, with horror, that the heatwaves would help the epidemic, and, at the same time, each person could see that summer was settling in. Above the city, the calls of swifts in the evening sky became shrill. They were no longer in keeping with these June dusks that make the horizon recede in our country. . . . It was clear to people that spring was exhausted, that it had lavished itself on the thousands of flowers bursting open everywhere, and that it would doze off now, collapsing slowly under the double heaviness of the heat and the plague. For all our fellow citizens, this summer sky, these streets paling under the shades of dust and boredom, had the same threatening aspect as the hundred dead who weighed down the city each day.[4]

As the North African summer looms, it becomes harder to distinguish between the weather and the symptoms of disease. The shadows cast by the hot sun become "shades," ghosts of the season's dead. The flowers of April and May

burst, scatter, and collapse like plague victims, sinking into
the season's exhaustion. Dr. Rieux has the impression that
"the entire city had a fever."[5] There's a brutal lushness to this
heat, a virulence that awakens both human desire and microbial life. Summer is the harsh season, and soon "under the
red July sky the city, packed with couples and shouts, drifts
into the panting night."[6]

II. THE WEATHER IN PLAGUE

It's a little-known fact that Camus worked briefly as a meteorologist. For almost a year, from 1937 to 1938, he wore a
lab coat at the Algiers Geophysics Institute and catalogued
measurements of atmospheric pressure from hundreds of
weather stations across North Africa. The data had been pil-
ing up, and despite the arrogance of their imperial ambitions,
the men who ran the institute couldn't attract enough fund-
ing. They didn't have the money to hire a scientist trained
for this "exacting and, in effect, stupefying task."[7] Nonetheless, Camus's supervisor, Lucien Petitjean, was pleased with
his work. By the end of his time at the institute, Camus had
plotted curves for twenty-seven years of barometric pressures from 121 weather stations. He also made calculations,
averaging monthly meteorological data. This work must have
given him a granular picture of the weather, one that was so
dry and clinical it was at odds with his experience of the natural world. "Like in all sciences of description (statistics—
which collects facts—) the biggest problem in meteorology
is a practical problem: that of replacing missing observa-
tions," he wrote in his notebook. "Temperature varies from
one minute to the next," he clarified. "This experiment shifts
too much to be stabilized into mathematical concepts. Observation here represents an arbitrary slice of reality."[8]

Soon Camus went to work for a newspaper, *Alger républicain*, leaving the Geophysics Institute behind. But his sensitivity to fluctuations in the weather stayed with him, especially when he decided to write about a plague. For the novel, he drew once more from a scientific source with literary connections—Adrien Proust's 1897 book *La défense de l'Europe contre la peste*. Proust was, as I mentioned, an epidemiologist and the father of the writer Marcel. Proust's volume is full of weather, and he carefully examines how the climate of different cities has affected their history with the plague. "*The seasons* exercise an influence over the development or the spread of these epidemics," he writes, signaling that "the temperature, the winds have a certain effect."[9] He describes the dry heat of Egypt, the humidity of Algeria, and the way certain storms might even accelerate disease.

Did the doctor's son pick up on this apprehension when he created his own literary obsession with weather reports and measuring barometric pressure? *In Search of Lost Time* is full of human barometers attuned to changes in the weather, and the narrator's father is first among them. The scholar Eve Kosofsky Sedgwick argues that for the narrator, Marcel, and for his father, these day-to-day alterations in weather are more than meteorological. "What does the narrator mean in calling himself an animated barometer?" she asks in *The Weather in Proust*. To be a barometer involves being able to gauge the weather, to measure it against past and present, to hold a kind of memory within yourself that might come back to haunt you in the future:

> For the narrator, waking from sleep to find changed weather is a way of being "born again." . . . And paradoxically, the very ordinary seriality of weather offers a kind of daily, ground-tone pulsation of the *mémoire involontaire*. . . . "Atmospheric changes, provoking

other changes in the inner man, awaken forgotten selves"; "we re-
live our past years not in their continuous sequence, day by day,
but in a memory focused on the coolness or sunshine of some
morning or afternoon."[10]

Sedgwick's brilliant passage reveals a link between the workings of involuntary memory and the idea of a human barometer. To Marcel Proust, and to his father figures, each day's
weather could be a trigger of involuntary memory, a point of
comparison between today's spring self and the lost self of a
previous spring. The weather is a daily reminder of similar
moments in past seasons, a "ground-tone pulsation" of cool
mornings where our present experience snags on our memories of the past. How many of us, during quarantine, experienced these kinds of moments ourselves, even in the form
of longing, dissonance? How many of us felt the softness of a
spring afternoon and had to force our bodies to think of the
pandemic, to stay wary?

III. SKY TRANSLATIONS

In April 2020, I spoke with a group of thirty-five medical
professionals in New York City who were reading *The Plague*
as hospitals were filling with COVID patients. To them, it
was clear that the character of Dr. Rieux was expressing
more than an individual perspective—*as he chooses to write
his chronicle,* one doctor said, *he becomes the voice of collective trauma.* In his years at the Algiers Geophysics Institute,
Camus himself had become something of a human barometer. And who better to carry that knowledge in his fiction
than Dr. Rieux, sensitive chronicler of both weather and illness? As we've seen, by giving his narrator a collective voice,
Camus sets himself apart from Proust's luxurious individualism. But Camus also left himself with a problem—how to

express emotions, mourning, desperation and maintain collectivity? One of his answers was to turn to the weather in plague as a form of collective experience, because everyone in the city is trapped under the same sky. In the most harrowing moments of the book, when Rieux is grappling with the deaths of those around him, he allows his internal feelings to merge with the weather, burying personal experience within natural phenomena that are visible to everyone in the city. These moments are like tiny memorials where Camus anchors human grief in the movements of the sky.

With the first death, the weather reflects a grim unease:

> The day after the concierge's death, large clouds filled the sky. Brief deluges of rain battered the city; a stormy heat followed these brusque showers. Even the sea had lost its deep blue, and under the misty sky, it took on shades of silver or iron, painful to see.[11]

At the moment the word "plague" is first spoken, Camus places it in direct contrast with the April sky:

> The doctor was still looking out the window. On one side of the pane, the fresh spring sky, and on the other side, the word that still resonated in the room: plague.[12]

After the death of a child, the exhausted Rieux looks up and sees the remaking of a bed:

> The heat fell slowly through the branches of the ficus. A whitish pillowcase was slipping over the blue sky of morning, making the air even more suffocating.[13]

After his wife dies, Rieux's mother waits for his reaction, but he is busy studying the sky:

> She looked at him but he stubbornly stared through the window
> as a magnificent morning rose over the harbor.[14]

These moments represent extreme feeling, but they also achieve their emotional pull through restraint. When the lens of the book expands to take in the sky, it encompasses a vast grief, translating a sadness that's too wild for the organized grid of a city and the ordinary language of politeness. Expressing loss as weather is a way of putting it where everyone can see it—somewhere unfinished, unresolved, unforgotten. After Rieux's best friend dies in the eleventh hour of the epidemic, the doctor learns that the administration will dedicate a monument to the victims of the plague. But that managed civic healing isn't where Rieux wants to locate his grief. Instead, as Alice mentions, he climbs to the terraces overlooking the city and the sea, to the place where he felt closest to his friend. While he's standing there, he lets the weather remind him of the night he talked with Tarrou:

> The great cold sky sparkled over the houses, and, close to the hills,
> the stars hardened like flint. This night wasn't so different from
> the one when he and Tarrou had come to this terrace to forget
> about the plague. The sea at the foot of the bluff was just a bit
> louder than it had been. The air was still and light, relieved of the
> dirty gusts that brought the lukewarm winds of autumn.[15]

The thing about being a historical chronicler is that you're always straddling the line between writing for the past and being needed by the future. But there's no guarantee that future readers will have experiences that call to mind what you have written. Walking around my city, lines from *The Plague* kept appearing, like the fat buds of flowers; the cold, golden light; the lukewarm wind. We can't forget what

Camus claims to offer us in this chronicle—"his knowledge of the plague and his memory of it, his knowledge of friendship and his memory of it, of knowing tenderness and having, one day, to remember it."[16] This grief-stricken existence is what Camus calls "a life without illusions."[17] Will we experience future Aprils and think of our quarantine walks, of the sun bursts after days of cloud cover? We are constantly translating the world into memory, but I seem to have calibrated my internal barometer to match the emotional weather of *The Plague*.

On a cold day in May, as the north wind blew down from Canada and a white sky stubbornly resisted the lengthening arc of the sun, our friends and neighbors decided to battle their cabin fever by writing descriptions of the sky in chalk on the pavement. It was a brief window into how others would recall these strange days, a vision of people kneeling on the pavement, gazing toward the clouds. *Cataract sky can't shake clear*, my husband wrote. I stood there looking up and imagined a future where I might feel a certain heaviness on spring days when the sky is white velvet, an involuntary trace of the ways this pandemic has collectively changed our lives. In a country where grief often goes unacknowledged, I hope that this year isn't lost time, that we don't fall back on illusions in these surface streets. Maybe the weather will keep us from turning a blind eye.

8 TOXIC CITY

Alice

Camus, who liked to say he learned everything he knew about philosophy from playing soccer, shared with his fellow citizens of Algiers a deep-seated hatred of the city's number one rival—Oran. Yet circumstances kept leading him to Algeria's second city, and it was there, in the anxious lead-up to World War II, that he began to think about *The Plague*.

Why Camus chose Oran for a setting is one of the most enduring questions surrounding the novel. He wanted *The Plague* to express the confinement and horrors of World War II, "the stifling air from which we all suffered, and the atmosphere of threat and exile in which we lived."[1] He could have set his novel in Paris, where he was living when the Occupation ended, for Paris had experienced every tragedy and contradiction of the war: a complete Nazi takeover of government, deportation, resistance, black market—all the elements that would enter his allegory. Oran had had a quieter war. With the rest of Algeria, it was part of the so-called free zone of Vichy France, and then, after Operation Torch in 1942, it became Allied territory. Compared with Paris, Oran, on the surface, was far removed from the events Camus was trying to capture. But what if the right question isn't whether Oran or Paris lent itself better to an allegory about World War II? What if the right question, the question for our time, is this one: What about colonial-era Oran was toxic enough to inspire the novel?

———

Camus traveled to Oran on several occasions in the late 1930s—to perform with his theater troupe on the municipal stage, to interview for a high school teaching job, to spend the weekends on the beaches with friends during the period when he was covering a trial a few hours to the southwest for *Alger républicain*.

He returned to Oran for his vacation in the summer of 1939. He now had personal reasons for being there, a romance with a girl named Francine Faure whom he'd met at the Algiers lycée where she was studying math. He was serious about her. In the fall, after he lost his job at *Alger républicain*, he would stay from time to time with Francine's family in their Oran apartment on the rue d'Arzew, above the arcades of a commercial district in the city center. Two years before he and Francine married, Camus became an unofficial member of a family that included Francine's widowed mother, a postal inspector, and her sister Christiane, a professor of literature at the start of a brilliant career. The Faures owned two adjoining apartments at numbers 65 and 67; eventually, Christiane moved into her mother's flat at 65, leaving 67, rue d'Arzew to the young couple. It can't have been easy living in close quarters with these women. Christiane was protective of her sister and suspicious of her suitor. A running joke in Camus studies: he chose Oran as his setting because he wanted to visit a plague on his in-laws.

"The Minotaur, or Stopping in Oran" had come to Camus quickly during those early trips to the city. He spared neither Oran's dusty streets nor its commercial soul, nor the bad taste on display in every boutique, nor the ridiculous sight of its overdressed young people strolling down the boulevard Gallieni—boys who wanted to be gangsters, girls who wanted to be American movie stars, and boxing fans who liked to brag before a match that there would be blood. Camus locates the city's violence in the ring, where romance and the ritualized equivalent of murder compensate for a life where nothing happens.

After the people, Camus turns to the monuments, each uglier than the next. Then he shifts tone entirely, with lyrical descriptions of the beaches along the cliff road, from Mers-el-Kebir to Bouisseville: "On these beaches of Oran each summer morning feels like the world's first."[2] I like to imagine that when Camus first cruised along the ocean highway in his friend Pierre Galindo's convertible, his scorn for the city center melted into wonder. Oran will always be two places for him: dust and scourge, beach and respite.

I visited that city and those beaches for the first time in the summer of 2012. My friends in Algiers told me I could hire a guide through Bel Horizon. Since 2001, the organization, proud of its independence from any cultural ministry or local government, has devoted itself to keeping alive all the many layers of the city's history through guided tours, community walks, and the conservation of the city's diverse memory sites. The guide assigned to me was one of the founders of the association, Abdeslem Abdelhak, and he quickly became my teacher. Abdel knows Camus's Oran by heart; he knows the writer's geography and every word he ever wrote about the city. He took me on Camus's walks through the center of town, past his favorite cafés and restaurants, from the waterfront to what remains of the old Spanish district. We stopped in a café not far from one of the ancient walls, where Abdel could imagine Rambert negotiating for his escape from the city. Oran sits directly across the Mediterranean from Alicante, Spain, a relatively quick ferry ride, even in the 1930s. According to a 1938 report by the French geographer René Lespès, Oran was 45 percent Spanish, and the Spanish accounted for 65 percent of the European population.[3] The Spanish near-majority in Oran would have been meaningful to Camus, whose mother's family came to Algeria from Mallorca. He points out in "The Minotaur, or Stopping in Oran" that only the Spanish neighborhood, the Quartier Marine, has an organic connection to the water. In *The Plague*, the Spanish outskirts of the city, with their modest one-story dwellings, have pride of place. Rieux goes there to treat the old man with asthma and finds him counting chickpeas. Rambert and Cottard meet with smugglers in the Spanish café to negotiate Rambert's escape, and later, Rambert lodges with Marcel and Louis at the edge of the district, near the gates of the city. Gonzales, Raoul, and Garcia are part of the cast of characters involved in Rambert's drawn-out efforts to escape. In the end, Camus wrote far more about Spanish Oran than he did about the commercial rue d'Arzew where he lived with his in-laws—as if the city center were too cold to contain the heart of his narrative.

Any history of Oran in the 1930s is incomplete without accounting for its fascist mayor. When Abdel first told me about Gabriel Lambert, we were on the rue d'Arzew, in a tiny lunch place serving *calentica*, a popular chickpea custard devised in Oran when Spain controlled the city. Lambert was a defrocked priest who came to Algeria in the 1930s with his dowsing rod and promised the people of Oran he would find them fresh water, which had always been in short supply in the drought-ridden climate. He wrote exalted accounts of his searches. Traveling through the desert, he felt his dowsing rod throbbing, electrified: "My dowser began to turn with a violence, at the same time as my body received a true nervous shock, like an electrical charge." He portrayed himself as a Christ figure with special powers that drained his psychic energies: "Those who, in the future, will benefit from my searches will not suspect, as they are watering their palm trees, the suffering this discovery cost me."[4] In an old newsreel, you can see him shaking a tiny dowsing rod that looks more like a rosary, while his long cassock trails along the sandy ground. His face was long and narrow, his nose set low, his ears set high—a "curious sinister figure," the voice-over says.[5] Everything about Lambert was flamboyant. He wore a priest's cassock and the standard settler's safari helmet, and with his skinny form, his wire rimmed spectacles, and his perpetual smile, he looked like a deranged schoolboy, not a dangerous troublemaker.

It wasn't long before Lambert's much-publicized search for water turned into a search for votes. He was elected mayor in 1934 on an inclusive, multicultural platform, promising support to Oran's large Jewish population and spouting paternalistic condescension at the Arabs—most of whom didn't have the right to vote. Eventually, his inspired search for water faded into a municipal project to link Oran's water supply to a dam in Beni-Bahdel, for which Lambert claimed credit. By then, a more dangerous transformation was in the works: when the Jewish community backed a Socialist candidate during the legislative elections of 1937, Lambert, still mayor of the town, ran for the legislature as well, in a time-honored accumulation of government posts that the French system allows. A Popular Front candidate with support from the Jewish community defeated him. When he failed to win a seat, he switched in a matter of months, via his pulpit as mayor, from philo-Semitism to virulent anti-Semitism, and his civic ideals took a clear fascist swerve.

Camus never mentions the Abbé Lambert by name, neither in fiction nor in essays nor in newspaper articles, but in "The Minotaur" he describes the aggressive blasting of stone, the dramatic public works undertaken with the support of the General Council and its most enthusiastic member, Mayor Lambert. On the orders of these officials, workers blasted an opening in old Spanish walls to give access to the route des Planteurs, leading out of the city along the beaches—the "cliff road" in *The Plague*. The mayor and his cronies commissioned plans for a waterfront boulevard so that Oran would no longer turn its back to the sea. And in the nearby Mers-el-Kebir, the Oran city government sponsored a massive project to make the port an official naval installation. There are harrowing descriptions in "The Minotaur" of the horror of colonial labor: "Scores of men, hanging from the same rope against the cliff face, their bellies pressed to the handles of pneumatic drills, quiver day after day in midair, unloosing whole patches of stone that crash down in a roar of dust."[6]

Gabriel Lambert understood these backbreaking public works as part of a fascist renewal of city life. He wasn't alone: by 1939, the swastika was visible all over Oran, as graffiti on the walls, on tie clips, even on packages of Bastos cigarette papers.[7] Camus paints Oran in *The Plague* through the allegory of a Nazi-controlled city; in fact, until 1940, the city was actually run by a politician who credited National Socialism as a profound source of inspiration.

In 1938, Lambert created a coalition of extreme-right political groups, the Amitiés Latines, or Latin Affinities. Its headquarters were at 62, rue d'Arzew. The Faures' apartments were at 65–67, rue d'Arzew. Lambert's propaganda office was directly across the street! It would have been impossible for the Faures, and for Camus, even on a short visit, to ignore the noise of would-be Algerian fascism.

But Oran was never Camus's political beat. By fall 1939, his newspaper *Alger républicain* was fighting with government censors. Camus, who had been an outspoken critic of Algiers city hall, was reeling from the declaration of war in September, which coincided in Algiers with the demise of his beloved newspaper and in Oran with the departure of Lambert, who was drafted into the French army. In the transition from "The Minotaur" to *The Plague*, Lambert faded into a bad memory. In the novel, Joseph Grand describes a more generic mayor whose strong suit is cheerful denial: "the mayor, a major captain of industry in our city, who vehemently insisted that when it came down to it (and he insisted on this phrase, which carried all the weight of reasonableness), when it really came down to it, nobody here was dying of hunger."[8] There are no political personalities in city hall; instead, government is systematically cruel. When Rambert tries to get official permission to leave the city, he finds offices where the "faces were as readable as filing cabinets or shelves of binders."[9]

———

"At first glance, Oran is, in fact, an ordinary town and nothing more than a French prefecture on the Algerian coast."[10] But first glances are deceiving. During the pandemic I traveled, masked, to the French colonial archives to take a look at the records of the Prefecture of Oran from the 1930s and 1940s. In the chaos of packing up in the French administrative exodus from Algeria after the war of independence, some papers made it to France; others didn't. Records from Algiers are scarce. But for Oran, there are thousands of documents, everything from the police commissioner's files, to intelligence reports on Jewish-Muslim relations, to complaints sent to the state prosecutor. And dossier after dossier on Lambert, the trouble he made, and the enthusiasm he inspired in French Algeria, especially among conservative nationalists. His popularity grew even greater after a disgruntled museum curator whom he'd fired retaliated by shooting him. The bullet pierced his lungs, but Lambert made a full recovery. His supporters put his plaster bust on their dining room tables. It must have seemed to his enemies as if he'd never leave.

An aficionado of pastis, Oran's liqueur of choice, the Abbé Lambert would roam the cafés at night with his bodyguard, his buddies, and his favorite women. On one of these evenings, he claimed to have been attacked by "a gang of little Jews" on the rue d'Arzew, Camus's street. He put up bright red posters all over the city, one of which stood out from the stack of yellowing papers in a box at the archives. He told his story, claimed his right to self-defense, and promised to avenge his attackers.[11] A member of the city council, appalled by the posters, wrote in protest to the public prosecutor. Lambert, drunk, had provoked the fight himself, and the so-called Jewish element was completely imaginary:

> I want to point out, Mr. Prosecutor, that this situation is bound to repeat itself and that my complaint must be made public so that Oran can regain its former calm. I want you to notice that when Mayor Lambert is out of town, Oran is calm.[12]

Lambert left town quite a bit, on so-called information-gathering trips to Benito Mussolini's Italy, Francisco

Franco's Spain, and Adolf Hitler's Nazi Germany. *Oran ma-tin*, the newspaper that supported him, published his 1938 dispatches from Germany, where, in the guise of reporting, he lauds the Nazis for their social progress, describing the anti-Jewish laws in enthusiastic detail.[13] He concludes that Hitler's government is offering a viable model for France. In Lambert's fascist vocabulary, France needed to draw on its Latin genius, the same way Hitler had consolidated Germany's Aryan genius. "Latin" was a quality claimed on the mainland by Charles Maurras, founder of the reactionary Action Française, but in Algeria, Latin was even more specifically racial, a code for European authority and the exclusion of Jewish and Arab natives.

Right under the arcades where Camus started writing *The Plague*, Lambert stoked the political fires with his propaganda: fascism instead of a popular front, corporatism instead of unions, and tying it all together, the fear and hatred of a Jewish enemy. A study of the Algerian Left based on the colonial records of the Oran Prefecture describes countless altercations between socialists and fascists between 1936 and 1940.[14] Camus wrote in support of the Blum-Viollette proposal that would have granted citizenship to a Muslim elite, a proposal that elicited Lambert's worst fears: "The Viollette project must be regarded with suspicion because it joins all those who promote the idea of an 'Algerian nation' that is not France, that does not want to be France."[15] In Lambert's French Oran, violence was verbal and physical—and not just in the boxing rings.

In the colonial archives in Aix-en-Provence, I was lucky to speak with the archivist Daniel Hick, who, through his work classifying the thousands of files, probably knows more about the administration of colonial Oran than any other living soul. He told me it would be hard to underestimate the unbridled violence and political tension in Oran during the terrible decade of the 1930s. And there was another aspect I learned about for the first time. He told me that Oran was called "the penitentiary department" of Algeria because of the number of camps and prisons established there by the colonial government. The summer of 1939, a refugee camp was set up in Ain-el-Turck, one of Camus's favorite beach towns. He was there that year, during his August vacation.

With the end of the Spanish Civil War, Oran created even more camps. Refugees came in droves from Alicante and crossed the Mediterranean in terrible sanitary conditions. They were the defeated Spanish Republicans—workers, intellectuals, stranded children. The municipality of Oran, which was fiercely anticommunist, feared them and considered their left-wing commitments a contagion. Every piece of paper in the public health files devoted to the refugees holds a painful human story—about the children, about the political activists who could never go home, about the literal diseases that broke out in close quarters.

One of those refugees touched Camus's life. The artist Orlando Pelayo came to Oran in March 1939, on the last refugee ship to leave Alicante, just before the port was taken by Franco's forces: "At dawn on March 29, 1939, the three thousand five hundred Spaniards who crammed into the old coal ship *Stanbrook* saw, emerging from the waters, a great cliff strewn with lights. Our eyes, accustomed to the darkness of a war, clung in amazement to those luminous promises of freedom."[16] Instead, after the twenty-hour trip across the Mediterranean, the ship waited in port while a panicked municipality decided the fate of its passengers. Expecting freedom from fascism, Pelayo instead spent two years in Oran detention camps. In 1941, finally freed from confinement, he settled in the city and began exhibiting his paintings at an

art gallery owned by one of Francine Faure's cousins. He soon
grew friendly with Camus. More than once, Pelayo remembered, when a refugee needed housing, Camus offered shel-
ter on the rue d'Arzew.

There was incarceration, too, for the native victims of a
typhus epidemic that struck the countryside around Oran
in 1941. Camus's friend Emmanuel Roblès, whose wife had
taken ill, told him about camps where natives who had
caught the disease were held in tents. "What's most original about our city is how difficult it can be to die there. Dif-
ficulty, though, isn't exactly right, and it would be better to
talk about discomfort."[17] Camus's remark is part environmental, part social. Oran's refugee camps and typhus camps
find their way into the novel: Rieux, Rambert, and Tarrou
are meeting after dinner in a small cramped bar in Rieux's
hotel, where the loud voices are a shock after the silence of
the infected city. Rambert is absorbed in his drinking, but
Rieux can't drown out the obnoxious talk drifting over from
a corner table, where a naval officer is discussing contain-
ment camps in Egypt, expressing the worst aspects of hy-
gienic colonialism:

> At one of the two tables that occupied the tight corner where they
> stood, a navy officer with a woman on each arm was telling a fat,
> congested listener about a typhus epidemic in Cairo: "Camps, they
> made camps for the natives, with tents for the sick and, all around,
> a perimeter of guards who fired on the families when they tried to
> sneak in homemade remedies. It was harsh, but fair."[18]

Camus doesn't mince words. You have to be despicable, and
heartless, to think that firing on native families when they
try to bring medicine to their ailing, incarcerated relatives
is "fair." Though Camus moved this example to Egypt, he

could have been talking about plenty of repressive and cruel policies that existed in colonial Oran, where native Algerians suffering from typhus were placed in camps. As for the camps in *The Plague*, Camus describes isolation in a municipal stadium, lined with tents, where sentries prevent the sick from leaving and the well from seeing what is inside. But it's the camps that Rieux doesn't see firsthand that haunt the city most:

> There were many more camps in the city that the narrator can't say anything about because of his scruples and because he has no firsthand information. But what he can say is that the existence of these camps, the smell of men that came from them, the huge voices of speakers in the dusk, the mystery of the walls, and the fear of these condemned places weighed heavily on the morale of our fellow citizens and added to everyone's distress and malaise.[19]

Laura's essay on restraint helps me think about this disturbing passage, where the fact of not claiming firsthand experience enables Rieux to evoke the unseen horror: the smell of the men who've been in the camps, the sound coming from loudspeakers that might be discernible, even at a great distance. In Oran and in Europe, people went about their daily lives, living next to these places of terror.

———

After the war broke out, Camus waited in Oran. Most of his friends had been drafted into the army, as Mayor Lambert had been, but Camus was ineligible because of his tuberculosis. His editor, Pascal Pia, found him a job in Paris. Mind-numbing work at a big daily, on the layout desk. And after

France fell to the Nazis, after he moved from Paris to Cler-
mont Ferrand to Lyon with the newspaper, he was laid off
shortly after his wedding to Francine, who had traveled to
the mainland to join him. The couple returned to Oran, and
it was there, from January 1941 to March 1942, that he suc-
cumbed to one of his worst bouts of tuberculosis, but nonetheless finished *The Stranger* and began to write *The Plague* in
earnest, returning to the criticisms of Oran that he'd begun
to develop in "The Minotaur." Again, he waited for special
permission from the administration to return to the mainland for his tuberculosis treatments.

Oran under Vichy was quieter, its tensions tamped down.
Lambert had left for the army, and when he returned after
the armistice, the Vichy government passed him over and
named a replacement. But quiet doesn't mean fair or just,
and you could say that as of 1940, Oran became an even more
toxic place. When Camus returned to city in January 1941, he
was painfully aware of how many lives had been turned up-
side down by Vichy's anti-Jewish statutes, with their special
mention of Algeria. In 1870, France decreed Jewish Algerians
citizens; in 1940, it stripped them of their rights by abrogat-
ing the Cremieux decree.

In Algiers and in Oran, in Camus's circle of friends and
acquaintances, there were Jewish teachers and Jewish students who had to abandon their work toward various de-
grees, and lycée and university professors ordered to vacate
their positions by December 1940. Students in primary and
secondary school, like Jacques Derrida, were dismissed from
their classrooms.

Camus had already given private tutoring in history and
geography before he left Oran for Paris in March 1940. When
he returned, he started teaching again in a private school
that his friend André Bénichou had opened to serve the Jew-

ish students. Bénichou was a philosopher who had lost his own job at the lycée in Oran. Camus taught unofficial classes to small groups of Jewish students scattered throughout various apartments in Algiers. On one of our walks, Abdel pointed out a building in the Jewish district and another one on the palm-lined street where, on a Saturday afternoon, the "Clarques" and the "Marlenas" would strut. I was moved to find, in an online blog, a remembrance by Paul Benaïm, who'd been a schoolboy in Oran during the 1940s. He wrote about a dining room converted to a schoolroom on the rue Étienne-Eugène, with a pale, taciturn teacher who knew a lot about literature. He can still remember seeing Camus wandering through town in a worn raincoat. He figured he was either depressed or ill.[20]

The place that horrified Camus most in his walks through the city was the Maison du Colon (the Settler's House), which was erected by the French to celebrate the centenary of French Algeria. Abdel shows me a fresco on the front of the building called *Mater Africa*, depicting a goddess whose head is enshrouded in a halo, receiving gifts from slaves. Those mosaics were so shiny, Camus wrote in "The Minotaur," that you might first be blinded to what they represent. *Mater Africa* interested him less, however, than another frieze hidden on the side of the building along what was once boulevard du Deuxième Zouaves. It's still there, as Camus described it, but you'd have to come armed with binoculars or a telephoto lens: a colonizer in his white shirt, white helmet, bow tie, and walking stick, his hands clasped in rest as the natives bend under their labors. A reminder of agricultural profit on the backs of the colonized.

Camus's sense of a toxic city is never stronger than in his description of the Maison du Colon: "Boldness of taste, love of violence, and a sense of historical synthesis. Egypt, Babylon,

and Munich have collaborated in this delicate construction —
a large cake resembling an immense inverted cup."[21] The political innuendo is in the details: when Camus wrote those
lines, Munich had become the site of the beer-hall putsch,
the capital of Nazism.

9 THE ESSAY GARDEN

Laura

"The heart wears out with sorrow and labor," Camus wrote in *The First Man*, "it forgets sooner under the weight of fatigue.... To bear up well you must not remember too much, but rather stick close to the passing day, hour by hour."[1] I understand this advice, but I also resist it. It feels like austerity for memory.

Sometimes it's easier to exist "hour by hour" in a place that isn't your own, to see, in your mind's eye, something other than the dark days of February in Buffalo, something besides the wind from the North tossing the branches, the air alive with snow. I never intended to stay in this city for uninterrupted months on end. I thought I'd travel, deepening my impressions of home as I returned again and again. Instead, the slow realizations of quarantine, the hollowing out of perception—as Camus writes of those stuck in Oran, "We knew that our separation was destined to last and that we had to try bargaining with time."[2] Well. Let me try a little bargaining.

———

Once, there were the parks of other cities, the borrowed apartments, the paths hidden and lost. There was the last place I went before the long stall—a greenhouse in the Jardin d'Essai du Hamma in Algiers, a greenhouse full of seedlings, tender under the clouded glass of a different century. Once I flew three thousand miles to see the condensation on the greenhouse in an Algerian park, in a month when it was still possible to watch algae streak across the panes of another world. This is no ordinary park, as Hélène Cixous writes of her childhood wanderings, but a garden with a capital "G," "the *Jardin d'essai*, a Garden in which both Derrida and I discovered all the essays that sprout in the ear and in the soul."[3]

I don't know what I expected one December day when I walked in the garden unaccompanied, down the alleys of giant plane trees whose leaves had half fallen, littering a clearing where two paths crossed. Park workers in green jumpsuits were sweeping the leaves with long brooms made of bundled sticks, spinning around to create circles of neatness. In the *buvette* beside the crossroads, I bought a little coffee in the kind of cup dentists use for mouthwash. It tasted like Nescafé. Sitting on a bench, I felt a clearing open, a broom-swept center that had been buried under leaves. My semester of teaching was over, and I had nothing in my pockets but the key to the apartment where I was staying and a little cash wrapped around my American driver's license.

Sometimes the fate of a garden can run parallel to the history of a country. During World War II, when Camus was writing *The Plague*, the Jardin d'Essai was requisitioned by the Allies, who occupied it and caused considerable damage. It was hit by aerial bombardments and partly destroyed when a battleship exploded in the bay right beside the park. For Cixous, the childhood innocence of the garden ended early. Her Jewish family in Algeria had their French citizenship revoked by Vichy, and the place became a "thorny version" of itself, "not the *Jardin d'essai*, but *Décès*: of death."[4] After the war, the gates of paradise don't exactly close behind her, but the park never looks the same: "The iron bars, *barreaux*, which mock the anagram of trees in French, *arbres*, climb towards the blue sky."[5] The bars of the garden show her sensitivity to who is being kept out, and an awareness of her own presence there. The *arbres* had to be rehabilitated from the bombardments, and the garden reopened in 1948, the same year the first translation of *The Plague* was published in Britain and America. Four decades later, the Algerian Civil War shut the gates again. The 1990s were Algeria's "black decade," when the army fought with the Islamists, and as many as two hundred thousand Algerian civilians lost their lives. During these dark years, the garden was closed and fell into disrepair. People were afraid of who might be hiding in its palms.

In the Allée des Dracaenas, the branches are so intertwined that you can't see their fronds exploding into the air above you until you step out from under their shade. Then they appear from the long, green shadows like dappled fireworks. For Cixous, the Jardin d'Essai is a garden attempt in the same way that an essay is an argument attempt—they share the same literal root. And the garden was built to make a point: as one of many public works during the colonial era, it grew within the fucked-up legacy of a civilizing mission. The earliest goal was to *assainir* a marshy patch of land, to make a "plagued" space into a nursery where varietals could be developed to feed, cure, and amuse the settler population. *Assainir* means "to clean up," "to make healthful, sanitary." As the writer Sofiane Hadjadj puts it, in 1847, the French director of the garden wanted to make "a spectacular leap forward, tripling its size, bettering the sanitation of the ground—on a particularly marshy site that had given its name to that part of Algiers, 'El Hamma,' 'the fever.'"[6] You can feel Hadjadj's irony here, in the way he paraphrases the ridiculous self-importance of the director's tone, the tone of spectacle and arrogance and conquest. The early French settlers in Algiers were preoccupied with marshes, places whose sediment-rich soil produced the odors and mists associated with miasma, and therefore with plagues. They didn't know a time was coming when marshes might save a city, filter its toxins, prevent the erosion of its streets.

On the hill above the park, the monument to the martyrs of the Algerian Revolution defines the sky-scape of the city. This garden was built for the wrong reasons, but now the memorial has reclaimed the view.

When I visited, the park was full of school groups—teenagers taking selfies, a small boy chasing pigeons, women eating lunch, fathers holding their kids' hands as they peered into the koi ponds, older children climbing in the ficus trees. Camus grew up on the street that runs past this park, and what was once Belcourt is now Belouizdad. It's still a working-class neighborhood—a man winked as two boys climbed the garden fence, avoiding the entrance fee.

When the sun came out, the tree shadows launched themselves across the pavement, entangling on the ground. That was the last time I was invited anywhere, the last time it was possible to travel for research, to pour myself into the details of someone else's life. Though I knew Camus had worked on *The Plague* while separated from his wife, for a long time, I didn't understand why the idea of exile was so pervasive in a novel about quarantine. For most characters, wasn't the lockdown of a city a case of entrapment at home? Yet Camus writes about it often:

Yes, it was the feeling of exile, that hollow we carried constantly within us, that precise emotion, the desire to go backwards or the opposite, to hurry the march of time, these burning arrows of memory. If, from time to time, we let our imaginations go and amused ourselves with waiting for the sound of the doorbell to return, the familiar step in the hall, if, in those moments, we consented to forget that the trains were stopped, if we arranged to stay home at the time when, normally, a traveler carried by the evening express might have arrived in our neighborhood, of course, these games could not last.[7]

Reading this, I understood that exile takes place in time as much as in location. Until you realize you're in the aftermath of a plague or a war, it's hard to see how much the time spent waiting, surviving, has changed the city around you. Sarah Schulman expresses this perfectly in her introduction to *Rat Bohemia*, about fighting against the AIDS epidemic in New York neighborhoods. "I stayed put," she writes, "and my home left me."[8] The longer an epidemic lasts, the more it enacts this form of exile. You can go nowhere and still, there is nothing familiar left.

––––––––

In quarantine, the Jardin d'Essai is closed again for the first time since the Algerian Civil War. In the absence of visitors, a false rumor circulated that the lions in its zoo were starving, leading the garden to turn its social media into a giant proof-of-life campaign. They assure their followers that the lions are fine—their photo appears with fat steaks tossed through the bars. But the comments remain skeptical. In the greenhouses, in the cages of the animals, light diffused through dust catches and flares on the lens of the professional photographer who has watermarked this lion portrait. It looks as carefully posed as a holiday card, and I'm sick of myself for being on this stupid app in the first place.

One memorable resident of the zoo in Hadjadj's novel is "an elderly lion, impressive and sad, who people say has gone blind because of some secret grief."⁹ As I read his book, it starts snowing in Buffalo. In a pandemic, it's always snowing, burying us under the same drift of accumulated minutes. People are dying, and whole books of misery are being written. Ghosts are walking the paths of our associations and, for better or worse, we're discovering the richness of our interior lives. But this essay isn't a pep talk or a photograph or a proof-of-life campaign. In my memory of that visit, the pandemic hadn't yet come to the Jardin d'Essai. I hadn't yet researched the marshes.

This essay is a guest on the bridge to an island of palms, while small boys chase pigeons, and goldfish swim through the arched shadow like coins with copper wings. Here lions go free in the park, breaking into the meat locker and gorging for days until their fur is golden and shiny and their bars no longer carry the smell of human handprints. This essay takes the train to Oran, a city named after lions, and watches the morning suburbs dissolve into fields of orange groves. Many things wake this essay from its cabin-fever dream.

10 THE ENDLESS SENTENCE

Alice

Grand is the patron saint of writer's block. But actually he isn't blocked, just dissatisfied with his words. He keeps rewriting the same sentence, hoping that a different adjective here, a pronoun there, will finally give him satisfaction. He's an individual word man, in the great tradition of Gustave Flaubert who wrote to Louise Colet in 1853: "We must pile up a mass of little pebbles to build our pyramids."[1] Or maybe he's more like Cratylus, who argues with Socrates that there's a perfect word for each thing. Grand studies Latin etymologies to understand the essence of his language. He's so concerned about his individual words, he doesn't really question his setting, his scene, his characters. He never asks why there needs to be a woman on horseback, why the flowers need to be in bloom, or why she's riding in the Bois de Boulogne.

Camus's problems in writing *The Plague* were different. He experienced work on the novel as a series of stumbling blocks, centered around the structure of his narrative and on his cast of characters rather than on individual words. Stephan, the suicidal classics professor from manuscript version one, came and went.

Camus reassigned his suicide to Cottard, whose name Camus borrowed from the doctor in Proust's *In Search of Lost Time*. In Proust, Cottard speaks in ridiculous clichés. In *The Plague*, Camus gives the clichés to Grand. Grand's search for the perfect word becomes even more poignant because he's prey to silly clichés and to the way people talk in his hometown of Montélimar, in the Drôme—the deep Midwest of France. Naïve about the world of publishing, he fantasizes that his editors will break out into a unanimous "Hats off!" if he succeeds. But he's also sophisticated in his ambitions; he knows the music of language counts, and he wants his description of the equestrienne to trot with a one-two-three phonetic rhythm. He doesn't realize that the one-two-three rhythm isn't a trot but a canter.

Making Grand homely, with his droopy yellow mustache and thin shoulders, prevents him from being a Hollywood-style hero. He shares plenty of other traits with Camus, who has distributed features of himself among the characters in his novel. Grand has tiny handwriting—Camus's own manuscripts are nearly illegible. And like Camus in his youth (meteorologist, tutor, layout editor), he works all sorts of odd jobs. He's perennially dissatisfied with his writing.

Grand is many things in *The Plague*, but above all, he must be a therapeutic element for the writer—an agent of Camus's own dissatisfaction with the novel he's writing. During his 1946 vacation, Camus wrote to his friend Nicola Chiaromonte: "I've just finished *The Plague*. But I am so far from finding this book good that I doubt I can let it be published. What good is it sharing my disappointment, which is so deep, with others?" In November of that year, he wrote: "I plunged back into *The Plague*, taking and reworking it in part. I can't stand the book anymore. And I'll give it to the editor this week, the way you get rid of something disgusting."[2]

Camus loves to create stories within his fictions that interrupt the straight line of the plot. In *The Stranger*, there is the drama of Salamano and his dog, the sighting of the automat woman, the clipping Meursault finds under his prison mattress about a mother who kills her own child. In *The Plague*, Tarrou's notebook provides a parallel account of the plague full of quirky stories, like the one about the man who spits on cats from his balcony. But Grand's struggle to tell a story is essential plague behavior—a strategy for survival. He makes us ask what purpose an imaginary world can fill amidst the horror. Can the horse and the beautiful equestrienne in the Bois de Boulogne cleanse our imaginations of disease and transport us to a perpetual spring? The scholarly edition of *The Plague* duly notes that there was a Bois de Boulogne in Algiers, near the area known today as El Mouradia. But when I read Grand's sentence, I don't see the local park—it never had any flowering alleys. I think of Proust's Bois, the playground of Charlus and Odette, and I imagine Camus reading Proust as a very young reader and wondering if a boy like himself from a spare, impoverished universe had any right to become a writer. The Proustian Bois was an exotic dream space for the toothless colonial settler who had to quit his studies to eke out a living as temporary municipal assistant. Grand earns sixty-two francs and three centimes a day because he never finds quite the right words to ask for his due.

When Grand succumbs to the plague, he tells Dr. Rieux to burn his manuscript—fifty pages of the same sentence written over and over, possible revisions "infinitely copied, reshuffled, lengthened or cut down."[3] Like Rambert, starting over and over again in his attempt to escape Oran, Grand, too, is Sisyphus, sentenced to an eternal repetition of the same struggle with words:

One fine morning in the month of May, an elegant equestrienne rode a superb sorrel mare down the flowering lanes of the Bois de Boulogne.

One fine May morning, a svelte equestrienne rode a superb sorrel mare down the flowering lanes of the Bois de Boulogne.

On a fine morning in May, a svelte equestrienne, mounted on a sumptuous sorrel mare, was riding, in the middle of flowers, the lanes of the Bois . . .

On a fine morning in May, a svelte equestrienne, mounted on a sumptuous sorrel mare, was riding, in the middle of flowers, the lanes of the Bois . . .[4]

At Gallimard, Camus's fellow editor Raymond Queneau published a book in 1947 called *Exercises in Style*—ninety-nine versions of a man getting on a bus. Grand's earnest attempts to improve his sentence have none of the confident playfulness of Queneau's pastiches, where each exercise represents a distinct mode of speech (official letter, free verse, exclamations). Still, Grand's equestrienne offers us a distraction from the tragedy of the epidemic. Written in a different state of mind, Grand's sentences might have been taken for an avant-garde experiment: take the most banal sentences imaginable and twist them into a thousand variants.

Rieux admires this unsung statistician who counts the victims of the plague, keeps going, and asks for no glory for himself: "Grand, more than Rieux or Tarrou, was the real example of the calm virtue that animated the public health squads."[5] Rieux doesn't trust heroism. But he concedes that if there has to be a hero in the fight against the plague, it would be Grand, "this insignificant, unassuming hero who had nothing going for him but a little goodness at heart and a seemingly ridiculous ideal."[6]

For Grand, the world of sentences in all their variety isn't divorced from the world of plague victims demanding to be tallied. He has flights of fancy in the midst of his numbing bureaucratic work. He refuses to abandon literary creation. At the same time, he won't give up his work on the plague, always endeavoring to find a clearer way to present the statistics that the public health squads need. He can turn any public space, office or infirmary, into a work space:

> He would set up there with his papers, the same way he set up at his post in city hall, and in the air thickened by disinfectants and the disease itself, he fanned the sheets of paper to dry the ink. He honestly tried, then, to stop thinking about his equestrienne and to do only what was required.[7]

Grand is also, of all the characters in the novel, the most openly vulnerable. There's a moment of intense communion between Rieux and Grand when Rieux sees him staring at a shop window, tears running down his face. Grand had once told Rieux how he became engaged to marry Jeanne in front of a shop window. Watching Grand remember losing Jeanne, Rieux can suddenly feel his own regrets about his absent wife. Rieux listens as Grand babbles, and that babble, the opposite of Grand's polished, endlessly edited sentences, releases a truer language. Grand confesses that he makes a terrible effort to be normal. Rieux takes Grand's hand and feels that it's burning. His friend has the plague.

Of all the characters in *The Plague*, the unassuming Grand has the happiest ending. To Rieux's astonishment, Grand is the first man on the public health squad to recover from plague. He's the first successful beneficiary of the serum. He manages to write to Jeanne, the wife he had neglected and who had left him years ago. And he announces with undisguised joy that he's removed all the adjectives from his sentence. Camus doesn't quote the stripped-down sentence, but we can imagine it: "An equestrienne rode a mare in the Bois." Grand's brush with death has burned away all the frills.

So Grand is comic relief, but he's never ridiculed. He's an anomaly in the novel, a writer and a bureaucrat and a survivor of plague, a source of admiration and deep sympathy, and the only person to whom Rieux reveals his own suffering. When he's sick with plague, Grand asks Rieux to burn his pages, but after he recovers, he's ready to start again. He remembers everything. Instead of burning his own manuscript, Camus sent it into production, but even as he sent it, he was sure it was a failure. Once the novel was published, he could only marvel at its success. As he liked to put it, *The Plague* had more victims than he could have anticipated. And so his profound dissatisfaction with the manuscript turned into a wry affection.

A year after *The Plague* appeared, Camus wrote to his Italian friend about a joke he'd taught his twins, Catherine and Jean. He and Francine called them "the two scourges":

> "Who is the Plague," I ask Jean.
>> "It's Cathie"
>> "Who is Cholera?"
> Cathie replies, "It's Jean."
> "Who is the victim?" And the two respond in unison: "It's Papa."[8]

11 ANTHOLOGIES OF INSIGNIFICANCE

Laura

Early on in *The Plague*, Dr. Rieux realizes that in order to fight against the disease in his city, he has to
resemble it a little. As he moves from house to house,
counts the dead, isolates the sick, and separates the
living, his exhaustion forces him to notice a creep-
ing indifference in the thick of things—his heart goes
numb and his personal life is subsumed by the plague
narrative. In his chronicle, too, the disease dominates,
and there are only a few moments when he steps outside its grasp. In practice, this means his narration al-
ternates between sections that tease out the existential dilemmas of the plagued city and sections where
his characters talk and move through the world. This
balanced pacing progresses from general to particular, contextualizing the details of each dramatic
scene. For a writer who has historical or allegorical
ambitions, this method is quite effective at creating
tension, dread, and suspense. But fortunately Camus
rebelled against the crushing power of the plague narrative, giving us not only Rieux's chronicle but also
Tarrou's.

When my favorite character enters *The Plague*, he's presented as "a historian of what has no history." It's possible to mistake this man for a dreamer, a poet with a capital "P," someone whose quoted notebooks are absurd, "biased toward insignificance." According to the narrator, Tarrou has "gone out of his way to examine things and people through the wide end of the binoculars."[1] He likes to jot down conversations he overhears on the tram or in the hotel restaurant. He eavesdrops on ordinary citizens as they speculate about their colleagues or forbid their children from discussing rats over lunch. He writes about the effects of the plague on a little old man who enjoys luring cats into the street underneath his balcony so he can spit on them "with force and precision." What's worse, "If one of his gobs hit its mark, he would laugh."[2] In the midst of a plague, laughing feels weird, unseemly. The narrator remarks that Tarrou's notebooks might be perceived in the same way, that his bias toward insignificance might lead readers to "suspect a dry heartlessness underneath."[3] But is insignificance heartless?

To get at the source of this question, let's look at an exchange between two actual poets. In the mid-1930s, after he fled Germany, Bertolt Brecht wrote a poem called "To Those Born After," which laments the heartlessness of going about ordinary life during dark times. The fact that the slightest everyday actions feel wrong is a sign of how deep the darkness really is:

> What kind of times are these, when
> A talk about trees is almost a crime
> Because it implies silence about so many horrors?
> When the man over there calmly crossing the street
> Is already perhaps beyond the reach of his friends
> Who are in need?[4]

For Brecht, crossing the street calmly or speaking about the natural world might make you complicit. Brecht's world resembles Rieux's, in that he feels tremendous guilt if his witnessing gaze is even briefly disrupted, if he steps outside the darkness for even a moment. In this sense, Tarrou's notebooks are suspect—insignificance runs the risk of appearing indifferent. But that isn't the whole story.

In 1995, Adrienne Rich published a poem called "What Kind of Times Are These," a poem whose title isn't a question, but a way of saying *well, if you have to ask.* Rich doesn't just borrow from Brecht's poem here—as someone born between before and after, she argues with the idea that her present moment is somehow divided from his darkness, that after can be anything but aftermath. "There's a place between two stands of trees where the grass grows uphill," she writes,

> I've walked there picking mushrooms at the edge of dread, but
>   don't be fooled
> this isn't a Russian poem, this is not somewhere else but here,
> our country moving closer to its own truth and dread,
> its own ways of making people disappear.[5]

To pick mushrooms at the edge of dread is to harvest what grows from the rot of forgetting, to excavate the silences around injustice, to examine the forces that make people want to turn to the topic of trees. Only by luring people into this wood, by noticing which way the grass grows, can she hope to remind a listener that they, too, live with history. And not the history of Germany, or Russia, or the darkness of some other country, but their own. "Because in times like these," she writes, "to have you listen at all, it's necessary / to talk about trees." For Rich, the gesture of turning to detail is anything but insignificant, since it disrupts the habit of not listening at all. Rich's response to Brecht is helpful because it presents insignificance as an *alternative* to indifference, a way for the trees to pull a listener out of self-absorption.

As a reader, it's hard to avoid the rebellious charm of Tarrou's notebooks, which enter the longer, more straightforward narrative of the plague chronicle just when the latter feels like it might be inescapable. As vignettes, Tarrou's entries disrupt the polished alternation of reflection and action to insert small flashes of all-too-human non sequitur. The manager of the hotel finds dead rats in the elevator and worries about the respectability of his establishment. The magistrate Othon is an "owl-man," whose children sniffle into their pâté like trained poodles.[6] The little old man calls "minet, minet" to attract the cats. But what begins as insignificance doesn't always remain so slight. The cat-spitter is "crestfallen" when his furry targets disappear:

> That same day, the little old man had come out on the balcony at the usual hour, had shown a certain surprise, bent over, peered down the furthest ends of the street, and resigned himself to wait. His hand banged softly against the railing of the balcony. He waited a little longer, let fall a little bit of paper, went back in, came out again, then, after a certain amount of time, vanished abruptly, shutting his French windows angrily behind him. Over the next few days, the same scene repeated itself, but you could read increasingly obvious signs of sadness and distress on the little old man's face. After a week, Tarrou waited in vain for his daily appearance, and the windows remained stubbornly closed on a very understandable grief. "In times of plague," the notebooks concluded, "it is forbidden to spit on cats."[7]

Why does this passage hit so hard in the midst of all the panic and sorrow? When people are dying, who cares about the eccentric habits of a little old man? Tarrou obviously does, and his chronicle argues that we should, too. In a sense, we're lured into this man's story with all the particularity of its details: the little bits of white paper that fall like butterflies, the puddled shadows the cats slink into, the eyes pale with sleep, the old man's mussed hair. It seems safe to emotionally invest precisely because this story promises to be insignificant. And yet, despite its arch tone, the moral of this story is devastating—even the most eccentric of habits isn't safe from the crushing narrative of an epidemic. The city kills the cats, as spreaders of fleas, to prevent them from bringing the plague bacillus into contact with humans.

The story of the magistrate's family, a ridiculous portrait in Tarrou's notebook, also becomes tragic. After his mother goes into quarantine, the boy appears again in the hotel restaurant, looking like "a little shadow of his father," withdrawn and dressed in black. These details that begin as insignificance end up foreshadowing: the boy's life is in danger, and his story ends with one of the most agonizing scenes in the novel, in which all the characters must bear witness to the horror of the plague. When we next see this boy, he's a patient in a hospital bed whose case is so dire that Dr. Castel uses his first serum as an experimental treatment, and Paneloux begins to question his faith after the death of this innocent child. But it matters that Camus chooses to introduce us to the boy through Tarrou's perspective. By turning his binoculars around, Tarrou actually fights for the life story of the boy rather than the death story, keeping our curiosity about other humans alive. Detail, individuality, eccentricity: in this case, these are all antidotes to being a statistic, a patient, a body at risk.

During 1943, one of the darkest years of the Nazi Occupation of Paris, Camus wrote his own anthology of insignifi-

cance in his notebooks. There, he compares the general sig-
nificance of getting married to the habit of turning a door
latch to the right or to the left. "My action is insignificant,"
he writes, "unless, in my case, that habit is connected to a
concern for preserving my energy, a taste for efficiency that
could reflect a certain will, a way of life, etc. In that case,
it would be much more important for me to turn my latch
a certain way than to marry."[8] Unlike marriage, which has
the social importance of being recognizable to everyone,
the door latch is only meaningful as individual particularity. In *The Plague*, Camus calls this a "personal life," the "sum
of small things that meant much to them without meaning
anything to other people."[9] Though this philosophy is deep
within Camus's idea of the absurd, it was also at the heart
of his problems with the novel and the ethics of representing a collective experience as an individual artist. When he
wrote out this thought experiment, he was in the middle of
reworking *The Plague*, trying to make the second draft better and more alive than the first. How much individual particularity should he include in his novel when the forces of
plague were so recognizable in every element of society? In
the heavy context of allegory, insignificance was a breakthrough—it left him with pieces of his story that had room
to accumulate surprising meanings, narratives that could try
to puncture the suffocating arc of plague.

It's not a coincidence that the character who collects this
anthology of insignificance in his notebooks is also the character who advocates against the death penalty. Toward the
end of the novel, Tarrou finally chooses to reveal his true
concerns to Rieux. We learn that Tarrou's father was a magistrate, that on the days when this man asked for his alarm
clock, he was waking up early to attend the executions of
those he had condemned. In this exchange, Tarrou reveals

that his father invited him to the trial of a man who had red hair and chewed the nails of his right hand in the witness box. Ever since he watched his father condemn this man, Tarrou spent his life fighting against everything that "for good or bad reasons, kills or justifies those who kill."[10] In this exchange, Tarrou delivers the fulcrum of Camus's allegory when he refers to those who kill to enact their forms of justice as "les pestiférés," "the plagued." Fighting the plague here means fighting the deepest evils of human nature. In a world where a father who loves train schedules can ask for his alarm clock so he doesn't oversleep an execution, "everyone carries the plague inside them, because no one, yes, no one in the world is immune." As humans, Tarrou argues, we can hope we carry the plague as antibodies, so we attack hate and injustice when we see it in the world. Recognizing our potential to do great harm is exhausting, but without this vigilance, we can't be safe from violent tendencies. Tarrou's attitude couldn't be further from indifference—he's someone whose happiness "forgot nothing, not even murder."[11]

Small hints at this underlying philosophy are buried in his anthologies of insignificance. There's even a hidden link between the killers and the killed. As I mentioned, Othon is "the owl-man," resembling an undertaker in his long, black coat. Like Tarrou's father, Othon is a magistrate, responsible for condemning other people to death. When Tarrou presents his own life story, what I'll call his radicalization, he refers to his father's victim as the little "red-haired owl." Othon isn't just called the owl-man as a joke, a caricature—he's an owl-man because he, too, is responsible for killing little red-haired owls. The harder you look at Tarrou's anthology, the more significant it becomes.

At this point, I can't avoid it any longer—I have to confess that Tarrou breaks my heart. He breaks Rieux's heart, too. His death just days before the end of quarantine feels like punishment, and in a sense, it is. As he contemplates his post-plague future, Rieux forgets himself for a moment. "Yes, he would begin again when the abstraction was over," he thinks, "and with a little luck. . . . But he opened the door in that same moment, and his mother came to meet him, saying that M. Tarrou wasn't feeling well."[12] In this moment, the doctor begins to think of the plague as an abstraction that will end, and almost in the same breath, in just a single ellipsis, he learns that his best friend is sick. By thinking of the plague as an abstraction, Rieux lets down his guard, and in the pages that follow, he is reminded, in the most painful way, of how real, human, and concrete this plague actually is. A plague can never be an abstraction when it takes human lives. And the fight never ends.

Tarrou has to teach the hardest lesson: insignificance is a gateway into human life, and it's also a gateway out. When Camus chose how to describe the pathology of the plague in his novel, he lifted a curious quote from *Précis de pathologie médicale* by the doctors Fernand Bezançon and André Philibert: "The pulse becomes feeble and death follows when an insignificant movement occurs."[13] In the notes to Camus's complete works, scholar Marie-Thérèse Blondeau writes, "You wonder if it was the adjective that caught Camus's attention, given the importance Tarrou accords to insignificance."[14] Here, I have to make another confession. The first time I translated this sentence, I used "slightest" instead of "insignificant," which would have been a serious lapse, one that betrays my resistance to one of the most radical ideas in this novel. To Camus, insignificance is also deliverance— the movement that brings mercy after a long and painful struggle. "Life has assigned insignificance as its purpose," he wrote in his notebook. "Hence the interest of the anthology. It practically describes not only the greater part of existence, that of little movements, little thoughts, and little moods, but also our common future. These days, it has the extremely rare advantage of being truly prophetic."[15]

"Truly, I live in dark times!" Brecht cries from the margins. In a pandemic, it hurts to look at the prophecies of insignificance. When painters make work that's too big, when the confines of their studios won't let them step back far enough to see the contours of their vast tableaux, they turn their binoculars around. Let's go back to the words, to the cats, to the way a door latch might offer a key to the human heart. All day I sit at my desk while out the window, the branches grow long and scraggly on the shadeless spring trees. My neighbor tends them, moving slowly with clippers, drinking a tallboy can of Bud. In the vacant lot next door, a group of men sit in lawn chairs with maracas, something soft on the radio. All day, the cars parked and passing. And poets who echo "Thus the days passed / Granted to me on this earth."

12 THE ENDS OF WARS AND PLAGUES ARE MESSY

Alice

Nowhere else in Camus's novel do you feel the chaos of history as strongly as in its last pages, after the gates open and the city gives in to celebration. Camus was in Paris the third week of August 1944, witness to the retreat of the German army and the arrest of collaborators. Walking through Paris was dangerous during the popular insurrection that broke out just before the arrival of General Philippe Leclerc's forces down the avenue d'Orléans. People were dancing in the street, women had their heads shorn for supposed acts of "horizontal collaboration" with German soldiers, and the last remaining Nazi sentinels abandoned their posts. You could hear the whizzing bullets of random snipers on rooftops during General Charles de Gaulle's triumphant march down the Champs-Elyssée on August 25. Paris was free, but the rest of Europe was still in battle—a limbo that lasted from the liberation of the capital in August 1944 until Victory day in May 1945.

Camus covered these events for *Combat*, and he also visited the other side of the Mediterranean, where a V-day parade by native veterans at Sétif, Algeria, ended in mass murder. It had begun in celebration. Indigenous Algerians who had fought on the mainland for France's freedom from Nazi Germany had been authorized to demonstrate on the condition that they wave only the French tricolor. Anticolonial feeling was high, and the men who had fought for France's freedom from the Nazis wanted to fly their own flag. A twenty-six-year-old Muslim scout carried an early version of the green and white banner that would become the symbol of an independent Algeria. The colonial police shot him dead. Panic and rioting ensued, and throughout the day, a hundred French, including the mayor of Sétif and a leader of the Communist Party—were mutilated, massacred. The army reported every European death in detail.[1] In the weeks that followed, the colonial government launched a bloody campaign of repression in eastern Algeria, massacring thousands of Muslims throughout the region. The numbers are contested, but they range from five thousand to forty-five thousand Algerian dead. Camus was one of the only French journalists to write openly about what had happened.[2] The so-called riot by the veterans was the beginning of a revolt. And out of that revolt came a revolution.[3] The end of one war was the beginning of the next.

Camus's articles for *Combat* about the crisis in Algeria alternated with his editorials about the purge of collaborators. Henry Rousso, whose books explore the changing French memory of the Nazi Occupation beginning with the purge, remarks how difficult it is to draw a line in time between the vigilante justice of the August days and the official punishments that took place over the next few years. These sentences were handed out by the various tribunals set up by the French Resistance Council in liberated Algiers. Among the many people accused of collaboration, government ministers were to be tried in a High Court; media personalities,

gangsters, and assassins in Courts of Justice in each department. Mundane collaborators—the Cottards of the real
world—were tried in Civic Chambers and sentenced to "national degradation." One in eight Frenchmen had files moving through the court system, but the number of cases that
actually went to court was much smaller.[4] Fifteen hundred
death sentences were carried out. The process known as "the
purge" began in October 1944 with the trial and execution of
a collaborationist journalist named Georges Suarez. By 1951,
it was over; the guilty were successively amnestied. The time
for forgetting had begun.

Not just forgetting, but the kind of commemoration that
erases the truth of suffering, as the old asthmatic in the novel
knows:

> "Say, doctor, is it true that they're going to construct a monument
> for those who died of the plague?"
>
> "The newspaper said so. A stele or a plaque."
>
> "I knew it. And there will be speeches."
>
> The old man gave a strangled laugh.
>
> "I can picture it by now: 'Our dead . . .' And then they'll break
> out the snacks."[5]

In France, as survivors of camps, veterans of resistance
movements, and dedicated members of political parties gath-
ered in their affinity groups, they renamed streets and put up
plaques to remember their dead. Political success in the postwar era was fertilized by these commemorations, and your
bona fides as an *ancien résistant* could get you far. In a 2003
comedy called *A Self-Made Hero*, an insignificant Frenchman
named Albert Delahousse (*housse* meaning "duvet" or "pillow
cover") infiltrates a reception for former free French Resistance fighters. He learns their codes and nicknames and con-

vinces them he'd actually been with them in London. Before he's found out, he's risen to the rank of lead military observer in the French Occupation zone in Germany. That's the comic version of false commemoration. The tragic version: it was standard practice in those early years to use the phrase "Mort pour la France" (Died for France) even on commemorative plaques for Jews who were deported to the death camps. The standard phrase for French war dead both betrays the truth about those deaths and spares the nation its responsibility. Mourning becomes ritual, as smooth as polished marble, and loss itself cannot survive its own official rhetoric. Camus evokes the false solemnity perfectly at the end of his novel: the commemorators intone "Our Dead" all the more quickly so they can get to the snacks on the buffet table.

In *The Plague*, we don't see Cottard on trial. Grand explains his suicide attempt at the beginning of the novel as the consequence of Cottard's "private sorrows," and it isn't until much later that he reveals that the police are investigating him for an old crime he thought had been forgotten. He's terrified of being arrested. "Odd duck" detectives come to interrogate him. On the day of the liberation festivities, he starts shooting out his window. He hits at least one policeman. But Camus saves the violent detail for a dog, maybe because, in the dehumanizing context of war, it's easier to feel pathos for this creature, "flipped like a crêpe, beating its paws violently to turn back over onto its side, shaken by long spasms."[6] The return fire by the forces of order crumbles Cottard's shutters. Finally, he is led out of his apartment building screaming, his hands tied. As the neighbors watch from their windows, a policeman, "with the full force of his fists," smashes Cottard's face.[7] Rieux can't get the image or the sounds out of his mind as he leaves the scene, and he decides that it's harder to think about a guilty man than a dead one.

The Liberation put Camus in the harsh light of day. As the editorialist for *Combat*, his positions on every social ill facing postwar France were hotly debated. The most immediate of these was the legal and ethical issue of how to punish collaborators. Camus entered into a passionate debate with a sixty-year-old journalist, the Catholic writer François Mauriac, a member of the conservative French Academy who had also published underground with the Éditions de Minuit. Camus and Mauriac exchanged salvos in their respective newspapers, *Combat* and *Le figaro*, their positions coming down to a choice between justice and charity, and a debate about which option would heal the nation better. Mauriac was closer to "truth and reconciliation" as a method of healing; Camus to a cleansing punishment that would remove the venom. Camus would always insist that he was committed to taking the side of the defendant—never the prosecutor. His 1942 novel, *The Stranger*, had taken the uncomfortable side of a murderer. Tarrou, with his story about his father waking to go to an execution, embodies that horror of prosecution. But there was a moment, before the Liberation, when Camus wrote in the underground *Combat* that Philippe Pétain's militia, by its own actions, had signed its death sentence—that the rotten branch needed to be cut out to save the tree.[8]

In January 1945, ill once again and preparing to take a month's leave from the newspaper, Camus published his strongest response yet to Mauriac's calls for charity. He deplored the tender concern he was hearing from some quarters as much as the cries of hatred he was hearing from others: "I see for our country two ways unto death (and there are ways of surviving that are no better than death): the way of hatred and the way of pardon. One seems to me as dangerous as the other."[9] If you eliminated both extremes, what was left? Camus had lost friends and comrades to Nazi violence. So for once—and it was an anomaly—he put his faith in the imperfect workings of human justice: there needed to be swift action taken in the courts to punish collaboration. He was soon disappointed, as the flaws of the purge trials became more and more evident.

By the end of the month, he seemed to change course. He agreed to sign a petition circulated among French writers asking de Gaulle to pardon Robert Brasillach. The writer and journalist had been sentenced to death after a six-hour trial. The prosecution had targeted his pro-Nazi propaganda; his written denunciations of communists, socialists, Jews, Catholics, Freemasons, and the Third Republic; and his participation in the cultural life of the occupiers—their German institute, their Rive Gauche bookstore. Brasillach had written, in a single terrible sentence that haunted him at his trial, that France needed to "separate from the Jews *en bloc* and not keep any little ones."[10] This was two months after eleven thousand Jews had been detained in the bicycle stadium (the Vélodrome d'Hiver, or "Vél d'Hiv") and sent to Auschwitz. Prime Minister Pierre Laval's official policy was to deport the children with their parents—he needed to reach a quota of deportations, and he suspected it would be bad for his image if there were too many Jewish orphans.

Camus wrote to the petition's organizer to make it clear he wasn't signing out of any solidarity for Brasillach. He disdained the man and his work. He wrote bitterly that Brasillach hadn't lifted a finger to save his own friends in the Resistance, the real Tarrous executed by the Nazis.[11] But with this signature, he returned to his core belief that the death penalty was a crime of the state.

The purge caused Camus to question his deepest beliefs about loyalty to the Resistance, and what kind of justice the country needed to build a new society. Eventually he admitted, in a lecture at a Dominican monastery, that Mauriac had been right.[12] In 1946, as he explored those issues in a series of articles in *Combat* entitled "Neither Victims nor Executioners," Camus scribbled this line in the work-in-progress notebook devoted in large part to *The Plague*: "A series of political texts around Brasillach."[13]

For a long time, I've wondered what Camus had in mind with this mysterious phrase. Simone de Beauvoir, describing Brasillach's journalism, his denunciations of Jews and Resistance fighters under threat, his calls to murder, concluded: "There are words as murderous as the gas chambers."[14] I wondered if Camus was saying that Brasillach *was* the plague he was making into an allegory.

But there's a more straightforward explanation, since in 1946 Camus began to curate a series of books for Éditions Gallimard, under the title Espoir (Hope). "We're in nihilism," Camus wrote, introducing the series. "We won't get out by pretending to ignore evil in our times or by deciding to deny it. The only hope is to name it instead, to inventory it in order to find the cure that ends the disease. This collection is just such an inventory."[15]

Roger Grenier, whose book on the purge trials, *Le rôle d'accusé* (The role of the accused), appeared in the series in 1950, liked to joke that Espoir was the most despairing, hopeless series of books imaginable. Camus's choices are eccentric, original. The first books in the collection were united more by a quality of voice, an unflinching look at pain, than by any kind of literary genre. Many of the books Camus selected were by women.

In 1946, the year he imagined "a series of texts around Robert Brasillach," Camus published Colette Audry's short stories, *On joue perdant* (Playing to lose); Violette Leduc's experimental novel *L'asphyxie* (In the prison of her skin), which refracts an abusive childhood in twenty-one scenes; and Jacques-Laurent Bost's quietly devastating *Le dernier des métiers* (The last profession), told by a doomed soldier in the Battle of France. Later, Camus discovered the posthumous manuscripts of Simone Weil, a writer in whom he recognized his own deepest moral aspirations.[16] He published eleven of her books, including *L'enracinement* (The need for roots), *La condition ouvrière* (The worker's condition), and *Oppression et liberté* (Oppression and liberty). Weil had lived by her ethics, no matter how uncomfortable, and died in a Surrey sanatorium in 1943, of the consequences of a self-imposed starvation coupled with tubercular lungs. She was Camus's *espoir*, a champion of the afflicted.

In the newspapers and magazines springing up at the Liberation, the Brasillach trial and execution produced polemic and analyses about the responsibility of the writer, from the Camus-Mauriac debate in *Combat* and *Le figaro* to Sartre's essay "What Is a Collaborator?," published in a Free French newspaper in New York, to Simone de Beauvoir's essay, "Eye for an Eye," in *Les temps modernes*.[17] An anthology of pieces might easily have come together as early as 1946 and been the occasion for a debate about how France should come to terms with what Camus was calling its "scourge."[18] If a writer could be killed for his words, then writing, and words, mattered. And if words could be responsible for the death of individuals, then could words also be a form of healing? If he was actually thinking about an anthology on the Brasillach case for his series, it remained a passing thought. The books in Espoir, with their desperate children and condemned soldiers, were also attempts to imagine, through fiction, memoir, and philosophy, a way out of war. The ending of *The Plague* is dark and violent. The bacillus lies in wait. And yet the bells are ringing, the lovers united, and the city and its survivors are looking to the future. Which is one reason why so many readers find *The Plague* a hopeful book.

———

Still. *The Plague* doesn't have a happy ending, despite the line that must be one of the most quoted of the novel, that there is "more to admire in humans than there is to scorn."[19]

Camus ends by playing with the convention of an ending: he promises endlessness. The plague is an ever-present threat—like totalitarianism, or any evil that lurks in the hearts of men: "The plague bacillus never dies or disappears. . . . It can lie dormant for decades in furniture and linens. . . . It waits patiently in rooms, in basements, in trunks, among handkerchiefs and paperwork."[20]

A footnote to the scholarly edition of the novel informs us that Camus's list was inspired by two of his sources: Henri Bourges, who wrote that plague could be transmitted via inert objects like linens, clothes, and merchandise, and Bezançon and Philibert, who write: "It can persist in natural environments (floors, linens, corpses) for a very long time, up to six months in certain conditions."[21] Camus's own list is just as ordinary, but it has a cadence and a symbolic weight that makes it unforgettable. The claim, too, is completely different. Unlike Bezançon and Philibert, Camus saw the afterlife of the plague as lasting far longer than six months—the plague bacillus is an eternal feature of the human condition. And the carriers of plague are everywhere. You could translate the French word *chambres* as both bedrooms and judicial or government chambers—it's hard to capture that paradoxical double meaning of the most private and most public of spaces into English. Was he thinking as well of the most murderous chamber of all, the gas chamber? Then there are trunks, emblems of travel but also time capsules stored in attics for safekeeping. In the images of handkerchiefs, there's the bloody handkerchief that must have been the first sign of Camus's tuberculosis. And, finally, perhaps the most significant of the list as far as Nazism is concerned: *paperasse*. Not just papers, but a mess of paperwork, of red tape. The tons and tons of papers collected from abandoned Nazi offices and assembled for the trial of the major war criminals at Nuremberg. The true responsibility for Western nihilism could not be adjudicated at Nuremberg, Camus wrote in *The Rebel*, because a court of law cannot condemn an entire civilization: "It judged on the basis of actions, for they at least cried out to every corner of the world."[22]

Paperwork as proof, trace, reminder. Not the hard-edged steles or plaques or official commemoration but the messy, fading evidence. The plague bacillus lasts forever, but our memory of the plague, how it came to pass, how it was stopped in its tracks, is forever threatened.

13 BLOOD MEMORY

Laura

One month before COVID, I walked through the streets of Oran, past the gates of the old Spanish walls, archways that close at the end of part 1 with a famous cliffhanger in the form of a telegram: "Declare a state of plague. Close the city."[1] As they do in the book, the gates of Oran open onto the road to the beaches, where Camus liked to swim, a respite from a city that felt unhealthy to him.

When he first fell ill with tuberculosis in 1930, Camus said that he had become "porous," sensitive to sound, sunlight, heat, subtle changes in color and shadow.[2] In fact, he had developed hyperesthesia—an increase in perception that is a documented symptom of the disease. At the time, Camus was only seventeen; before he spiked a fever and coughed blood, he liked school, the beach, and playing soccer. Without permission, without warning, his body had opened itself to a dangerous pathogen. He had become both a host of the tuberculosis bacillus and an unlikely guest in the realm of the sick and dying. As he lay in his hospital bed, he read the stoic philosopher Epictetus, who argues that we cannot change what the world throws at us, but we can shape our own sense of justice, of right and wrong. In this model, the mind is a vessel full of breath, and thoughts enter it as beams of falling light.

After undergoing pneumothorax, a treatment that involved collapsing the affected lung so that it could heal, Camus recovered and was allowed to return to school the following year. But coming out of isolation meant that beyond the fevers, the sweats, the exhaustion, he had to cope with the sense that he was a pariah, a vector of the "white plague," someone marked for early death. These perceptions of tuberculosis patients hurt his career. He wasn't allowed to take his qualifying exams to become a philosophy teacher. After that first bout, though he hoped for a cure, he never forgot that the disease was still dormant within him. A little overwork, too many cigarettes, a chill after swimming in the sea—these things could tip the balance inside his body between immune resistance and relapse.

When Camus finished the manuscript of *The Stranger*, he wrote to his future wife that "it was already completely traced within me."[3] But his infection meant that *The Plague* was already traced within him, too. As early as 1935, metaphors for illness begin to appear in his notebooks, particularly when he describes childhood recollections as "latent memory . . . (a glue that sticks to the soul)."[4] Here, "latent" is a curious choice, precisely because of its relationship to the dormant periods of an illness like TB. As a metaphor for potential recurrence, latency is a powerful way of describing what might be carried in human memory. Camus's early poverty, his images of his mother, his sense of silence and unexpressed emotion—all these elements of his childhood emerge again and again in his fiction. "Latent memory" implies a sense of lurking danger in recollection, a certain heaviness, but also the potential to rediscover the blueprint of a past struggle, knowing how to fight something because you know you've fought it before.

Bringing the biology of the immune system into the space of art could express layered political histories. At the cellular level, latent memory is related to the way white blood cells "remember" and produce antibodies to fight the illnesses they've battled in the past. At the time, the *Journal of the American Medical Association* described latency this way: "Latent infection, generally speaking, means the residence in the body of a specific infectious agent without any manifest symptoms. . . . After complete recovery from an infectious disease the infectious agent may survive in the patient for a variable time, sometimes for years, without causing any obvious disturbances. Here the infection outlives the disease."[5] Ideas like these fueled fears of asymptomatic transmission and contributed to the othering and surveillance of people who were perceived to have different histories of immunity, especially in the colonial era.[6] By choosing illness, and specifically latent illness, as his metaphorical system, Camus represented an epidemic with complex and far-reaching implications. When he turned to *The Plague*, he didn't just reference war through the allegory of illness, he represented the human potential for nationalism and violence through the idea of latency, an infection that outlives each individual outbreak of the disease. And latency gave Camus a pretext to draw from his intimate lived experience.

In the novel, Oran becomes quarantined, isolated, exiled from the rest of the world because of its outbreak of plague. Camus represents the city as a body: Oran is "a healthy man whose thick blood suddenly revolts."[7] That was his own experience of falling ill with tuberculosis, generalized into the text of his fiction. Though he applied it to a civic body, Camus

understood this blood revolt on a personal level. In 1942, just
as he was starting to work on *The Plague*, he could no longer
escape the bacillus that had been dormant within him. He
relapsed severely, undergoing pneumothorax on the opposite lung. Confined to his bed, to his apartment, to his least
favorite Algerian city, he couldn't swim anymore. In fact, he
couldn't even proofread his forthcoming manuscripts. After
1942, he was feverish in Oran, feverish in Paris, and feverish in America, when he was one of the first French writers to visit New York City after the war. A bizarre thought
crossed my mind: if Camus had been subject to the ther-
mometer checks some countries have been using to screen
travelers during the COVID pandemic, he would have been
turned away.

––––––––

In 1976, the Brazilian artist and chemistry professor Letícia Parente made herself an early vaccine passport. In her
video, she appears alone in a lab, injecting shots she has devised for "anti-racism," "anti-cultural colonialism," "anti-
political mystification," and "anti-art mythification." After-
ward, she makes a note of each vaccine in the official travel
documents required to leave the country.[8] You never see her
face, only her hands and the surface of her skin. This piece
is an early example of BioArt, a practice in which artists use
living forms, biological research, and scientific processes to
make their work. Parente's video also stemmed from her job
as a chemistry professor, and the camera focuses on the real
process of immunization—the cotton swabs are dipped in al-
cohol, her hands carefully draw the vaccine into the syringe,
then the needles are flicked with precision to tap out the air.
Parente creates a ceremony that is both intimate and civic:

through each jab into her skin, she excises one element of the sickness in her country. The video, *Preparação II*, makes explicit what is implicit in *The Plague*—that protection from harmful forces within human society develops on an individual basis, and that only by circulating in the world as an immunized human can you contribute to the safety of those around you. But immunity is never absolute. As Tarrou puts it, "we must watch over ourselves endlessly so that we are not led, in a moment of distraction, to breathe into another's face and give him the infection."[9] This vigilance is a form of herd immunity: the way a group of individuals can help eradicate a disease by developing antibodies through the use of vaccines. If enough people in a society vaccinate themselves against a disease—or a social ill—they prevent it from spreading, protecting individuals who are immunocompromised or otherwise susceptible to infection.

Herd immunity also protects those who can't afford to get sick. In the novel, disease is not an equalizer—it affects everyone, but not to the same extent. The poor neighborhoods of the city have their trash picked up much later, exposing them to more rats. These families also experience price gouging and food shortages, while the rich want for almost nothing. As Camus knew, plagues and wars do disproportionate damage, and only by avoiding these events can the most vulnerable groups be protected.

At present, it's not hard to imagine how disease resembles injustice, but Camus's idea that a plague could be an allegory for the Nazi Occupation was not always well-received. In the first months of the pandemic, I wrote a piece for the *New York Times* about the novel. In it, I referred to Sartre's famous 1970s quip: "When I think of Camus claiming, *years later*, that the German invasion was like the plague—coming for no reason, leaving for no reason—*quel con*, what a fool!"[10]

But Camus took a long view of war and fascism in *The Plague*, one that enabled him to think about how individuals could come together in the future to form a community that would protect them against forces like nationalism and hate. In his speech "The Human Crisis," delivered at Columbia University in 1946, he once again used metaphors of illness, calling hatred and indifference "symptoms" of lingering conflict. Unlike many of his contemporaries, he implicated himself and his country in the spread of this illness: "And it's too easy, on this point, simply to accuse Hitler and say that the snake has been destroyed, the venom gone. Because we know perfectly well that the venom is not gone, that each of us carries it in our own hearts."[11]

In response to the symptoms of war, Camus saw shared consciousness as a healing force, becoming particularly interested in how people could develop a global collectivity that would protect them against nationalism and fascism. While he knew that people carried traces of hatred, Camus was also hoping those traces could be transmuted into cultural antibodies that would help people recognize hate and fight back when they encountered it. In that same speech in 1946, he called for creating "communities of thought outside parties and governments to launch a dialogue across national boundaries; the members of these communities will affirm by their lives and their words that this world must cease to be the world of police, soldiers and money, and become the world of men and women, of fruitful work and thoughtful play." Writing *The Plague* in the form of a historical "chronicle" was a hopeful gesture, implying human continuity, a vessel to carry the latent memory of war as an inoculation against future armed conflicts. As Romain Gary wrote about Camus in his introduction to *The Plague*, "Perhaps he was pessimistic enough to think that all of us are stricken, but optimistic enough to feel that education, moral progress and some other unknown element that for lack of a better word I shall call human destiny could overcome the ever-present enemy in our blood."[12] Camus's idea of community resistance hinged on the idea that people in the future might be aware of the details of past violence, that memory might provide a kind of herd immunity to protect against the worst human tendencies, bringing him far closer to Parente than to Sartre.

But let me explore Camus's metaphor of blood revolt a little further. In *The Plague*, one of the key treatments to stop the epidemic is the serum Dr. Castel develops over the course of the novel.[13] Unlike vaccines, which encourage the body to develop its own antibodies, serums transfuse antibodies from recovered patients directly into the bodies of those who aren't yet immune. To rephrase it in the terms of Camus's allegory, a serum is a direct vehicle for redistributing the tools of successful resistance throughout a community. A serum takes one person's blood memory and shares it with others so that they can recognize and resist social ills in the future. There's an intimacy to this transfer, and a sense that no one can truly know if another person's revolt will be successful. After Dr. Rieux injects Tarrou with the serum, he speaks to the mystery of following another person's internal fight: "Tarrou's solid shoulders and powerful chest were not his best weapons, but rather the blood that had just spurted out with Rieux's needle, and, in this blood, what was more intimate than the soul and what no science could bring to light."[14] Here the allegory takes place, not on the scale of the plagued city, but through the medium of the blood itself.

In this choice of medium, Camus was ahead of his time—a literary BioArtist *avant la lettre*. By 2010, the artist Kathy High's Vampire Study Group was using science to bring these intimacies of the blood to light as a political vehicle for art about immunity. For her, the body's defense system could be violent and territorial as well as lifesaving. She created a piece in which participants are invited to have their blood drawn by a professional phlebotomist.[15] Then the white blood cells responsible for immunity are separated from the rest. Two people's white blood cells are placed in a single petri dish, where they battle it out to see whose immune response will "win." The winner then goes up in the bracket, into a new petri dish to fight someone else. Under the microscope, the two groups of white blood cells flicker under the lens like dystopian fireflies. "Blood is a powerful medium," High says in the trailer for the project. "Blood is a political medium. And blood is a potentially pathological medium." High came to this project out of a fascination with the mechanisms of her own immune system—like Camus, she has a chronic illness, but unlike his tuberculosis, her Crohn's disease has an autoimmune element. Her white blood cells are the partial cause of her symptoms. For her, a revolution in the blood can damage the host as much or more than a pathogen does. Immunity can turn on itself, and the body can attack its own.

———

Remarkably, Camus came to understand the dangers of immunity, too. In the aftermath of World War II, Camus ultimately came to recognize that by taking lives, the Resistance movement he had been a part of could start to perpetuate injustice, it could start to weaken the ethics of its own civic body. In this same vein, the scholar David Carroll argued that with the plague allegory, Camus

> explicitly dramatizes the limits that he was convinced needed to be accepted by all resistance movements, no matter how oppres-

sive and deadly the political plague being combated. It was when
no limits were placed on the means being used that the form of
resistance to one form of the plague became in fact the carrier for
the next form, the means of resistance themselves rapidly spreading the disease they were meant to combat.[16]

In Camus's mind, immunity could turn into autoimmune
disease, destroying the fragile balance that might allow a
postwar society to heal. Through the character of Tarrou, the
novel's resident activist against the death penalty, Camus de-
lineates where the blood revolt crosses over into revulsion.
As Jacqueline Rose writes in her brilliant essay on the novel:

> He is pointing the finger at the modern state, which forbids vio-
> lence to its citizens, not because, as Freud puts it, "it desires to
> abolish it, but because it desires to monopolise it, like salt and
> tobacco." For Tarrou, the responsibility of the citizen for his own
> violence is not diminished by such fraudulence but intensified,
> since it confronts him with what the state enacts in his name.
> The plague will continue to crawl out of the woodwork—out of
> bedrooms, cellars, trunks, handkerchiefs and old papers—as long
> as human subjects do not question the cruelty and injustice of
> their social arrangements. We are all accountable for the ills of
> the world.[17]

In the context of World War II, Camus's allegory gained him
all kinds of accolades. *The Plague* was a bestseller at home
and abroad. But as the forties gave way to the fifties and the
Algerian War intensified, his stance against revolutionary
violence satisfied no one. His friends on the Left backed
the Front de Libération Nationale as they fought for freedom from French rule. When it came to supporting independence, Camus chose the wrong side of history. Nineteen

fifty-seven was a polarized year—he won the Nobel Prize, but he also relapsed. Ostracized and in quarantine, he said that he had an ache in Algeria, as a patient has an ache in the lungs.[18]

That year, he published his last work of literary BioArt, a story called "L'hôte," which means both the host and the guest in French. In Camus's case, the word "host" is also epidemiological, the term for something or someone carrying a disease. In the story, which takes place on the high plateaus of Algeria, a French constable orders a French schoolteacher to bring an Arab prisoner who has killed his cousin to the authorities in the next village. After offering his prisoner hospitality, the teacher decides to free him in the mountains, hoping to exempt himself from participating in the violence of the colonial justice system. As the teacher feels revulsion toward both the prisoner and the constable, "a sudden anger against this man, against all men and their filthy spite, their inexhaustible hatreds, their bloodlust,"[19] it becomes a kind of disgust at his whole species. Who is the host in this scenario, and who is the pathogen? Camus refuses to say. What's certain is that despite his attempts to generalize, the teacher is not exempt—he ultimately signs the paper the constable asks him to sign; he's complicit, a member of a society that makes him sick.

———

We are all accountable for the ills of the world. But you can't inoculate yourself against something if you don't recognize it as a disease. In our own pandemic year, the confluence of COVID and Trump has thrown some of the latent infections lurking within America's memory into stark relief. Our institutional racism. Our enormous disparities in access to healthcare. Our unconscionably high rates of poverty and hunger. Our propensity for guns and vigilante killing. But plenty of people still want to look away. As Jacqueline Rose writes, "The plague sparks a revolution in the blood. It erupts like a protest or insurrection, a fleeting moment of lucidity. Seen in this light, the novel could be issuing a warning, or asking a question that is driving many responses to the world laid bare by COVID-19. Under what conditions can the truth of social deprivation be seen?"[20] When bias and hatred and deprivation are clearly visible, what will it take to provoke an immune response from the most privileged members of our body politic? What would it take for them to revolt against the suffering of others?

On a rainy day, we drove to Rochester to get the vaccine at a Walgreens. At the pharmacy, several others were waiting. Some were talking about shopping, going back to restaurants. Two men who looked like they had come in from the countryside were talking about their neighbor who had died. Her husband survived, they said, but what was he going to do now?

We stood still for a moment in the fluorescent light. Then one by one we all rolled up our sleeves and took the needle in the arm.

SOURCES

As we write this coda, our plague has neither died nor disappeared. New variants, waves, and breakthrough infections have brought home Camus's idea that we live with the danger of illness, that we always have. While some cities cautiously reopen, and the lucky ones revert to old habits, we think of Rieux after Oran's quarantine lifts, remembering "that this delight was always threatened. For he knew what the joyous crowd did not, and what you can read in books."

Since it was first published in 1947, hundreds of books and articles have been written about Camus's plague. What we've included here spoke to us while we worked on *The Plague* during the pandemic years of 2020 and 2021. We were particularly interested in the way Camus's novel has been discussed by people who either read it for the first time or returned to it within the past two years. The selections below provide more sources about Algeria, about Camus's life and work, about plagues, about reading *The Plague* in a pandemic.

FOR MORE ON ORAN AND ALGERIA:

Aissaoui, Rabah, and Claire Eldridge. *Algeria Revisited: History, Culture, and Identity*. London: Bloomsbury, 2017.

Cixous, Hélène. *Volleys of Humanity: Essays, 1972–2009*. Edited by Eric Prenowitz. Edinburgh: Edinburgh University Press, 2011. See, in particular, the essays "The Names of Oran" and "How Not to Speak of Algeria."

Djebar, Assia. *Algerian White: A Narrative*. Translated by David Kelley and Marjolijn de Jager. New York: Seven Stories Press, 2000.

Djemaï, Abdelkader. *Camus à Oran*. Paris: Michalon, 1995.

————. *La vie (presque) vraie de l'Abbé Lambert: Roman*. Paris: Le Seuil, 2016.

Hadjadj, Sofiane. *Un si parfait jardin*. Photographs by Michel Denancé. Marseille: Le Bec en l'air, 2007.

Metair, Souad, and Guillermo Igual. "Minas y gallerias: El sistema defensivo subterráneo de la plaza de Orán." *Revista aldaba*, no. 43 (2018): 231-48.

"Oran, une ville d'Algérie." Special issue of the journal *Insaniyat: Revue algérienne d'anthropologie et de sciences sociales* 23-24 (2004). https://journals .openedition.org/insaniyat/5334.

Raza Kolb, Anjuli Fatima. *Epidemic Empire: Colonialism, Contagion, Terror, 1817-2020*. Chicago: University of Chicago Press, 2020.

Tamalet Talbayev, Edwige. "Hybridizing the Myth, Allegorizing Algeria." In *The Transcontinental Maghreb: Francophone Literature across the Mediterranean*, 37-78. New York: Fordham University Press, 2012.

White, Owen. *The Blood of the Colony: Wine and the Rise and Fall of French Algeria*. Cambridge, MA: Harvard University Press, 2021.

FOR MORE ON CAMUS'S LIFE AND WORK:

Benhaïm, André. "Entrez, je suis pendu." *French Forum* 34, no. 3 (Fall 2009): 39-55.

————. "Poétique de l'insignifiance: Les anecdotes d'Albert Camus." In *Albert Camus au quotidien*, edited by André Benhaïm and Aymeric Glacet, 177-95. Lille: Presses Universitaires du Septentrion, 2013.

Camus, Albert, and Maria Casarès. *Correspondance, 1944-1959*. Paris: Gallimard/ NRF, 2017.

Carroll, David. *Albert Camus the Algerian*. New York: Columbia University Press, 2007.

Duclert, Vincent. "La mesure, seule maîtresse des fléaux: *La peste* de Camus." *Esprit*, March 23, 2020.

Gary, Romain. Introduction to *The Plague*, by Albert Camus, x-xiii. Translated by Stuart Gilbert. New York: Time, Inc., 1962.

Gray, Margaret. "Layers of Meaning in *La peste*." In *The Cambridge Companion to Camus*, edited by Edward J. Hughes, 165-77. Cambridge: Cambridge University Press, 2007.

Grenier, Roger. *Albert Camus: Soleil et ombre*. Paris: Gallimard, 1987.

Hawes, Elizabeth. *Camus: A Romance*. New York: Grove Press, 2009.

Kaplan, Alice. *Looking for "The Stranger": Albert Camus and the Life of a Literary Classic*. Chicago: University of Chicago Press, 2016.

Lançon, Philippe. "Peste!" *Libération*, July 27, 2009.

Lévi-Valensi, Jacqueline. *La peste d'Albert Camus: Essai/Dossier*. Paris: Gallimard Foliothèque, 2003.

Lottman, Herbert. *Albert Camus: A Biography*. New York: Doubleday, 1979.

Merton, Thomas. *Albert Camus' "The Plague": Introduction and Commentary*. New York: Seabury Press, 1968.

Pelayo, Orlando. "Los cuadernos de viaje: Mis recuerdos de Oran y de Albert Camus." *Los cuadernos del Norte*, no. 35 (January-February 1986): 50–55.

Rosenzweig, Gabriel. "Les premières éditions en espagnol de *La peste* et *L'étranger*." *Chroniques Camusiennes: Publication de la Société des Études Camusiennes* 32 (January 2001): 16–22.

Sanyal, Debarati. "Concentrationary Migrations in and around Albert Camus." In *Memory and Complicity*, 56–98. New York: Fordham University Press, 2015.

Spender, Stephan. "Albert Camus, Citizen of the World: His New Novel of Man at the Crossroads Pleads for Real, Universal Brotherhood." *New York Times*, August 1, 1948.

Todd, Olivier. *Albert Camus: A Life*. Translated by Benjamin Avry. New York: Knopf, 1997. Note that the translation is abridged from the French original.

Zaretsky, Robert. *Albert Camus: Elements of a Life*. Ithaca, NY: Cornell University Press, 2013.

———. *A Life Worth Living: Albert Camus and the Quest for Meaning*. Cambridge, MA: Harvard University Press, 2016.

———. "The Logic of the Rebel: On Simone Weil and Albert Camus." *Los Angeles Review of Books*, March 7, 2020.

———. *The Subversive Simone Weil: A Life in Five Ideas*. Chicago: University of Chicago Press, 2020.

FOR MORE OF CAMUS'S OWN WORK:

Algerian Chronicles. Edited by Alice Kaplan, translated by Arthur Goldhammer. Cambridge, MA: Harvard University Press, 2013.

Camus at "Combat": Writing, 1944-1947. Edited by Jacqueline Lévi Valensi with a foreword by David Carroll. Translated by Arthur Goldhammer. Princeton, NJ: Princeton University Press, 2006.

The First Man. Translated by David Hapgood, New York: Vintage, 1996.

"The Human Crisis." In *Speaking Out: Lectures and Speeches, 1937-1950*. Translated by Quintin Hoare. New York: Vintage, forthcoming.

"Letters to a German Friend" and "Reflections on the Guillotine." In *Committed Writings*, edited by Alice Kaplan, 1–98. New York: Vintage, 2020.

"The Minotaur, or Stopping in Oran" and "Nuptials." In *Personal Writings*, edited by Alice Kaplan, 119–45. New York: Vintage, 2020.

The Myth of Sisyphus, and Other Essays. Translated by Justin O'Brien. New York: Vintage, 1991.

Notebooks, 1935-1942. Translated by Ryan Bloom. Chicago: University of Chicago Press, forthcoming.

Notebooks, 1942-1951. Translated by Justin O'Brien. New York: Knopf, 1965.

The Plague. Translated by Laura Marris. New York: Knopf, 2021.

The Rebel. Translated by Anthony Bower. New York: Knopf, 1993.

The Stranger. Translated by Matthew Ward. New York: Knopf, 1988.

FOR MORE ON PLAGUES:

Bezançon, Fernand, and André Philibert. *Précis de pathologie médicale*. Paris: Masson, 1935.

Boccaccio, Giovanni. *The Decameron*. Translated by G. H. McWilliam. London: Penguin Classics, 2003.

Bourges, Henri. *La peste: Épidémiologie, bactériologie, prophylaxie*. Paris: Masson, 1899.

Cole, Lucinda. *Imperfect Creatures: Vermin, Literature, and the Sciences of Life, 1600-1740*. Ann Arbor: University of Michigan Press, 2015.

Croissante, Pichatty de. *A Brief Journal of What Passed in the City of Marseilles, While It Was Afflicted with the Plague, in the Year 1720*. London: J. Roberts, 1721.

Defoe, Daniel. *A Journal of the Plague Year*. London: Penguin Classics, 2003.

Manaugh, Geoff, and Nicola Twilley. *Until Proven Safe: The History and Future of Quarantine*. New York: MCD/Farrar, Straus and Giroux, 2021.

Mathieu, Monsieur le Chanoine. "Le choléra." In *La vierge de l'Oranie au XIX siècle*, 5-20. Oran: Imprimerie D. Heintz, 1900. Reprinted Hachette/Livre BNF, 2012.

Procopius. *History of the Wars*. Vol. 1. Translated by H. B. Dewing. Loeb Library of the Greek and Roman Classics. Cambridge, MA: Harvard University Press, 1914.

Proust, Adrien. *La défense de l'Europe contre la peste*. Paris: Masson, 1897.

Thucydides. *History of the Peloponnesian War*. Book 2, sections 47-54. Translated by Rex Warner. London: Penguin Classics, 1972.

FOR MORE ESSAYS ON *THE PLAGUE* SINCE COVID-19:

Daoud, Kamel. "*La peste*: Un manuel de dignité." *Le point*, March 10, 2020.

Dyer, Geoff. "The Existential Inconvenience of Coronavirus." *New Yorker*, March 23, 2020.

Hoberman, J. "America Infected: The Social (Distance) Catastrophe." *Paris Review*, March 16, 2020.

Jouet, Mugambi. "Reading Camus in Time of Plague and Polarization." *Boston Review*, December 7, 2020.

Marris, Laura. "Camus's Inoculation against Hate." *New York Times*, April 16, 2020.

Rose, Jacqueline. "Pointing the Finger." *London Review of Books* 42, no. 9 (May 7, 2020): 3-6.

Schillinger, Liesl. "What We Can Learn (and Should Unlearn) from Albert Camus's *The Plague*." *LitHub*, March 13, 2020.

ACKNOWLEDGMENTS

We'd like to thank the many people who helped us with this book, generously sharing their time during a difficult pandemic year.

We are especially grateful to the people and organizations who shared their knowledge of Oran and Algeria with us, including Abdeslem Abdelhak for his expertise in Oran's history and his photos of the Maison du Colon; Bel Horizon; Sarah Bouchakour for traveling with us to Oran; Ameziane Ferhani; Pierre Gillon and Caroline Van Wynsberghe for inviting us to share our work in progress; Djamel Hachi; Selma Hellal; Sofiane Hadjadj; Elisabeth Leuvrey and Abed Abidat at the MaisonDAR in Algiers and Père Guillaume Michel at the Centre Pierre Claverie in Oran for hosting us; Gabriel Rosenzweig for his helpful correspondence; Samir Toumi; and Catherine Corm-Kammoun, Grégor Trumel, and the Institut Français d'Alger.

At the Camus Estate, we'd like to thank Catherine Camus and Elisabeth Maisondieu-Camus, as well as Alexandre Alajbegovic for his help and advice. We are grateful to the Estate and the Wylie Agency LLC for permission to print excerpts from two unpublished letters by Francine Camus—to Nicola Chiaromonte, dated December 31, 1942, and to Germaine Brée, dated October 1, 1964; © The Estate of Albert Camus.

At the University at Buffalo Libraries, Michael Kicey provided excellent help with the bibliography and with research in a pandemic.

We're deeply appreciative of our family, friends, and colleagues who took the time to read all or part of this book in manuscript, especially Walid Bouchakour, Livia Bokor, Julia Dzwonkoski, Devika Jutagir, Matt Kenyon, Dolores Hayden, and Marly Rusoff. The three anonymous readers for the University of Chicago Press provided excellent feedback as we completed our final revisions.

Thanks to Raymond Gay-Crosier for his correspondence; to Paul Vanouse and the Coalesce BioArt Lab for their help with the final chapter; to the people and institutions who invited us to discuss our work in progress, including Julia Elsky at Loyola University Chicago; Nellie Hermann at the Columbia University program in Narrative Medicine; Dr. Barry Wu, Dr. Tosin Adeyemo, and Deanna Calvert at the Yale School of Medicine; Devin Lau at the Yale Center Beijing; Maureen Jameson and Laura Chiesa and their students at the University at Buffalo; and Mitch Pinkowski at Episcopal High School. We'd also like to thank Alice Kaplan's students and her co-instructor Maurice Samuels in their lecture course The Modern French Novel and the members of her graduate seminar, Translation Controversies, for their insights and engagement.

We'd like to acknowledge the editors and publications where ideas from this book first appeared. Laura Marris's essay "Atmospheric Changes" was published in *The Point*, with thanks to John Palattella, Rachel Wiseman, and Jon Baskin.

Initial versions of two paragraphs in the book originally appeared in her essay "Camus's Inoculation against Hate," which was published in the *New York Times Book Review*, with thanks to Emily Eakin and Pamela Paul.

Finally, we're grateful to the wonderful team at the University of Chicago Press, including Randolph Petilos and Levi Stahl. We're particularly indebted to our editor, Alan Thomas, for his insight and for giving us the nudge to write this book.

NOTES

PREFACE

1. René Etiemble, "Peste ou péché," *Les temps modernes* 26 (1947): 911. Albert Camus, "Letter to Roland Barthes on the Plague," in *Lyrical and Critical Essays* (New York: Vintage, 1970), 338-39. Translation edited for clarity.

CHAPTER 1

1. Albert Camus, *The Plague*, trans. Laura Marris (New York: Knopf, 2021), 7. Unless otherwise noted, citations to *The Plague* reference the Marris translation. Full publication details are given for all sources at first mention in a chapter, with short citations thereafter.
2. Albert Camus and Louis Guilloux, *Correspondance, 1945-1959*, ed. Agnès Spiquel-Courdille (Paris: Gallimard, 2013), 88. The phrasing is slightly different in the published novel: "it is time for Doctor Bernard Rieux to admit he is its author," 322.
3. *The Plague*, 77.
4. *The Plague*, 126.
5. Rigoberta Menchú, *I, Rigoberta Menchú: An Indian Woman in Guatemala*, edited and introduced by Elisabeth Burgos-Debray, trans. Ann Wright (London: Verso, 1984), 1.
6. *The Plague*, 323-24.
7. Daniel Secretan, "Le Portugal sous le régime de Salazar," *Combat*, April 23-24, 1945.
8. Albert Camus, *Notebooks, 1942-1951*, trans. Justin O'Brien (New York: Knopf, 1965), 147, translation edited.
9. Francine Camus to Germaine Brée, January 10, 1964, box 5, folder 1, Germaine Brée archive, Wake Forest University, my translation. Unless otherwise noted, sources in French are translated by Kaplan and Marris.

10. *The Plague*, 331.

11. Albert Camus, *The Rebel: An Essay on Man in Revolt*, trans. Anthony Bower (New York: Vintage, 1956), 22.

CHAPTER 2

1. Albert Camus, *The Plague*, trans. Laura Marris (New York: Knopf, 2021), 8.

2. Adrien Proust, *La défense de l'Europe contre la peste* (Paris: Masson, 1897), 6. Available online at https://gallica.bnf.fr/ark:/12148/bpt6k4414581 .texteImage.

3. *The Plague*, 66.

4. *The Plague*, 8.

5. *The Plague*, 212.

6. *The Georgicks of Virgil, with an English Translation and Notes*, trans. John Martyn (London: Printed by R. Reily, for T. Osborne, in Gray's-Inn, 1746), book 4, lines 475–85.

7. *The Plague*, 11.

8. *The Plague*, 188–89.

9. *The Plague*, 274–75.

10. *The Plague*, 275.

11. Natalie Angier, "The Wonders of Blood," *New York Times*, October 20, 2008.

12. Angier, "Wonders of Blood."

13. *The Plague*, 276.

14. *The Plague*, 276.

15. *The Plague*, 309–10.

16. *The Plague*, 276.

17. Members of the Ocean Memory Project, including John Baross, Peter Bradley, Lisa D'Amour, Jody Deming, Mandy Joye, Daniel Kohn, Christine Lee, Rebecca Rutstein, Heather R. Spence, Monique Verdin, Timothy Weaver, and Anya Yermakova, "The Ocean Carries Memories of SARS-CoV-2," *Scientific American*, August 15, 2020.

18. "Ocean Carries Memories."

19. Idir Bitam et al., "Zoonotic Focus of Plague, Algeria," *Emerging Infectious Diseases* 12, (December 2006): 1975–77.

CHAPTER 3

1. Emmanuel Macron, speech to the French Republic, March 16, 2020. For a full transcript in English, see "Emmanuel Macron's Speech to the French Republic," French American Chamber of Commerce, https://www.faccnyc.org /news/emmanuel-macrons-speech-french-republic, accessed October 28, 2021.

2. Albert Camus, *The Plague*, trans. Laura Marris (New York: Knopf, 2021), 78.

3. Albert Camus, *Notebooks, 1942–1951*, trans. Justin O'Brien (New York: Knopf, 1965), 60.

4. Francine Camus to Nicola Chiaromonte, December 31, 1942, box 2, folder 5, Nicola Chiaromonte Papers, 1921–1982, General Collection, Beinecke Rare Book and Manuscript Library, Yale University.

5. Camus, *Notebooks, 1942–1951*, 38. O'Brien translates: "Caught like rats."

6. *Camus at "Combat": Writing, 1944–1947*, ed. Jacqueline Lévi-Valensi, trans. Arthur Goldhammer, intr. David Carroll (Princeton, NJ: Princeton University Press, 2002), editorial on the tragedy of separation, dated December 22, 1944, 140.

7. *The Plague*, 11.

8. Albert Camus, *The Myth of Sisyphus, and Other Essays*, trans. Justin O'Brien (New York: Vintage, 1991), 15.

9. *The Plague*, 316.

10. *Camus at "Combat,"* December 22, 1944, 149.

11. Camus, *Notebooks, 1942–1951*, 123.

12. Albert Camus, *La peste: Le manuscrit d'Albert Camus* (Paris: Editions des Saints Pères, 2020). This is a facsimile of the first version of the manuscript.

13. Lucette Maeurer to Albert Camus, October 3, 1942, Special Collections, Raymond Gay-Crosier Albert Camus collection, Smathers Library, University of Florida at Gainesville, courtesy Raymond Gay-Crosier.

14. *The Plague*, 20.

15. *The Plague*, 143.

16. *The Plague*, 176.

CHAPTER 4

1. Albert Camus, *The Plague*, trans. Laura Marris (New York: Knopf, 2021), 272.

2. *The Plague*, 167.

3. Albert Camus, *La peste*, in *Œuvres completes*, ed. Jacqueline Levi-Valensi (Paris: Gallimard, 2006), 2:142.

4. Anjuli Fatima Raza Kolb, *Epidemic Empire: Colonialism, Contagion, and Terror, 1817–2020* (Chicago: University of Chicago Press, 2020), 140.

5. Jacques Derrida, *Acts of Religion* (London: Routledge, 2002), 68.

6. *The Plague*, 272.

7. Albert Camus, "Letters to a German Friend," trans. Justin O'Brien, in *Committed Writings* (New York: Vintage, 2020), 10. (The original French edition was published in 1948.)

8. W. G. Sebald, *On the Natural History of Destruction*, trans. Anthea Bell (New York: Random House, 2003), 57–58.

9. Albert Camus, *The Plague*, trans. Stuart Gilbert (New York: Knopf, 1948), 257.

10. *The Plague*, trans. Marris, 41.

11. Albert Camus, *The Plague*, trans. Robin Buss (London: Penguin, 2002), 31.

12. Albert Camus, *The Stranger*, trans. Matthew Ward (New York: Vintage, 1988), 122. I have modified the translation of *tendre* (Ward uses "gentle").

13. Albert Camus, *The Rebel*, trans. Anthony Bower (New York: Vintage, 1991), 292–93.

14. Albert Camus, "Nuptials at Tipasa," trans. Ellen Conroy Kennedy, in *Personal Writings* (New York: Vintage, 2020), 69.

15. *The Rebel*, 271.

CHAPTER 5

1. Albert Camus, *The Plague*, trans. Laura Marris (New York; Knopf, 2021), 129-30. Albert Camus, *Notebooks, 1935-1942*, trans. Philip Thody (New York: Knopf, 1963), 139, translation edited.

2. In a note to his unfinished autobiographical novel *The First Man*, trans. David Hapgood (New York: Vintage, 1996), 311, Camus imagines alternate chapters in the mother's voice, "commenting on the same events but with her vocabulary of 400 words."

3. *The Plague*, 312.

4. *The Plague*, 295.

CHAPTER 6

1. Albert Camus, *The Plague*, trans. Laura Marris (New York: Knopf, 2021), 186.

2. Decree by the French Consulate General in Oran, October 25, 2009, https://oran.consulfrance.org/Arrete-ministeriel.

3. Albert Camus, "The Minotaur, or Stopping in Oran," in *Personal Writings*, ed. Alice Kaplan (New York: Vintage, 2020), 126.

4. Farid Benramdane, "De l'étymologie de *Wahran*: De *Ouadaharan* à Oran," *Insaniyat* / 2004) 24-23 إنسانيات)), http://journals.openedition.org/insaniyat /5690.

5. Ibn Hawqal, *The Faces of the Earth*, 977. Cited in Benramdane, "De l'étymologie." The passage does not exist in the English translation of Hawqal.

6. Ahmed Abi Ayad, "Oran, l'Espagne et Cervantes," *Insaniyat* / 24-23: إنسانيات 2004)), http://journals.openedition.org/insaniyat/5636; https://doi.org/10 .4000/insaniyat.5636.

7. For more on the history of the Village Nègre, see René Emsalem, "Les villages indigènes d'Oran," *Revue de géographie jointe au Bulletin de la Société de géographie de Lyon et de la région lyonnaise*, vol. 25, no. 4 (1950), https://doi.org /10.3406/geoca.1950.5429. Camus mentions this place in *The Plague*, when Rieux walks there with Rambert.

8. "Shitty colonial period."

9. Camus, "The Minotaur," 125-26.

10. Souad Metair and Guillermo Igual, "Minas y gallerias: El sistema defensivo subterráneo de la plaza de Orán," *Revista Aldaba*, no. 43 (2018): 246.

11. Albert Camus to Roland Barthes, January 11, 1955, published in *Club*, the magazine of the Club du Meilleur Livre.

12. Debarati Sanyal, "Concentrationary Migrations in and around Albert Camus," in *Memory and Complicity* (New York: Fordham University Press, 2015), 57.

13. *The Plague*, 190.

CHAPTER 7

1. Albert Camus, *The Plague*, trans. Laura Marris (New York: Knopf, 2021), 250.

2. *The Plague*, 209.

3. Le Chanoine Mathieu, "Le choléra," in *La vierge de l'Oranie au XIX siècle* (Oran: Imprimerie D. Heintz, 1900), rpt. Hachette Livre/BNF, 2012, 5.

4. *The Plague*, 118–19.

5. *The Plague*, 34.

6. *The Plague*, 128.

7. Lewis Pyenson, "Habits of Mind: Geophysics at Shanghai and Algiers, 1920–1940," *Historical Studies in the Physical and Biological Sciences* 21, no. 1 (1990): 188.

8. Albert Camus, *Notebooks, 1935–1942*, trans. Philip Thody (New York: Knopf, 1963), 98, edited.

9. Adrien Proust, *La défense de l'Europe contre la peste* (Paris: Masson, 1897), 119.

10. Eve Kosofsky Sedgwick, *The Weather in Proust* (Durham, NC: Duke University Press, 2011), 8. Quotations within the block quote are from *In Search of Lost Time*.

11. *The Plague*, 33–34.

12. *The Plague*, 43.

13. *The Plague*, 232.

14. *The Plague*, 313.

15. *The Plague*, 330.

16. *The Plague*, 312.

17. *The Plague*, 312.

CHAPTER 8

1. Albert Camus, *Notebooks, 1942–1951*, trans. Justin O'Brien (New York: Knopf, 1965), 53.

2. Albert Camus, "The Minotaur, or Stopping in Oran," *Personal Writings*, ed. Alice Kaplan (New York: Knopf, 2020), 140.

3. René Lespès, *Oran* (Paris: Alcan, Collection Centenaire de l'Algérie, 1938).

4. Gabriel Lambert, *Journal d'un sourcier dans le sud saharien* (Alger: Editions Chaix, s.d.), 4.

5. Getty Images newsreel with voice-over in English, showing clips of Abbé Lambert in the desert and in political meetings. "Water Diviner," Getty

Images, https://www.gettyimages.com/detail/video/priest-abbe-lambert
-in-robes-w-pendulum-walking-w-men-news-footage/509486681, accessed October 29, 2021.

6. Camus, "The Minotaur," 137.

7. Benjamin Stora, *Les trois exils: Juifs d'Algérie* (Paris: Stock, 2006), 62.

8. Albert Camus, *The Plague*, trans. Laura Marris (New York; Knopf, 2021), 50.

9. *The Plague*, 113.

10. *The Plague*, 3.

11. "I'm not a sheep who can be easily slaughtered" (Je ne suis pas un mouton qu'on égorge facilement), from Abbé Lambert's poster, sent by the Chef de la Sûreté Départementale to the prefect of Oran, September 18, 1937, in FR ANOM 92/2531, Dossier Abbé Gabriel Lambert, 1936 to 1953, Archives Nationales d'Outre-Mer, Aix-en-Provence.

12. Letter to the prosecutor of Oran from a city council member, September 16, 1937, in Dossier Abbé Gabriel Lambert, 1936 to 1953, FR ANOM 92/2531.

13. L'Abbé Gabriel Lambert, *Allemagne, 1938* (Oran: F. Plaza Imprimerie, 1938).

14. Claire Marynower, *L'Algérie à gauche (1900–1962): Socialistes à l'époque coloniale* (Paris: PUF, 2018).

15. Abbé Gabriel Lambert, *L'Algérie et le projet Viollette: Conférence faite à Paris le 1er février 1937*, Oran: Imprimerie F. Plaza, 1938.

16. Orlando Pelayo, "Mis recuerdos de Oran y de Albert Camus," *Los cuadernos del Norte*, no. 35 (January–February 1986): 50–55. With thanks to Gabriel Rosenzweig.

17. *The Plague*, 5.

18. *The Plague*, 165.

19. *The Plague*, 260.

20. Paul Benaïm, "Quand Albert Camus enseignait le français à Oran," Morial, 2011, https://www.morial.fr/index.php?option=com_content&view=article&id=207:paul-benaim&catid=66:temoignages-ecrits&Itemid=462.

21. Camus, "The Minotaur," 134. With thanks to Abdeslem Abdelhak for his photographs of the frieze in 2021.

CHAPTER 9

1. Albert Camus, *The First Man*, trans. David Hapgood (New York: Vintage, 1996), 80.

2. Albert Camus, *The Plague*, trans. Laura Marris (New York: Knopf, 2021), 74.

3. Hélène Cixous, "How Not to Speak of Algeria," in *Volleys of Humanity: Essays, 1972–2009*, ed. and trans. Eric Prenowitz (Edinburg: Edinburgh University Press, 2011), 162.

4. Cixous, "How Not to Speak," 162.

5. Cixous, "How Not to Speak," 163.

6. Sofiane Hadjadj, *Un si parfait jardin*, with photographs by Michel Denancé (Marseille: Le bec en l'air, 2007), 63.

7. *The Plague*, 74.

8. Sarah Schulman, *Rat Bohemia* (Vancouver: Arsenal Pulp Press, 2009), x.

9. Hadjadj, *Un si parfait jardin*, 39.

CHAPTER 10

1. Gustave Flaubert to Louise Colet, March 27, 1853, in *The Letters of Gustave Flaubert: 1830–1857*, trans. Francis Steegmuller (Cambridge, MA: Harvard University Press, 1980), 182.

2. Albert Camus to Nicola Chiaromonte, August 27, 1946, 66–67, and November 14, 1946, 77, in *Correspondance, 1945–1959*, ed. Samantha Novello, (Paris: Gallimard, 2019).

3. Albert Camus, *The Plague*, trans. Laura Marris (New York: Knopf, 2021), 283.

4. *The Plague*, 110, 143, 144, 282.

5. *The Plague*, 142.

6. *The Plague*, 146.

7. *The Plague*, 146.

8. Camus to Chiaromonte, February 1, 1948, 3, in Novello, *Correspondance*.

CHAPTER 11

1. Albert Camus, *The Plague*, trans. Laura Marris (New York: Knopf, 2021), 26.

2. *The Plague*, 28.

3. *The Plague*, 26.

4. Bertholt Brecht, "To Those Born Later," *Bertolt Brecht Poems 1913–1956*, ed. John Willett and Ralph Manheim (London: Methuen, 1987), 318–20. I've modified the translation of the title in the text from "later" to "after," as it is currently translated.

5. Adrienne Rich, *The Dark Fields of the Republic* (New York: W. W. Norton, 1995), 4.

6. *The Plague*, 30–31.

7. *The Plague*, 120–21.

8. Albert Camus, *Carnets*, cahier 4: January 1942–September 1945, in *Œuvres completes*, ed. Jacqueline Levi-Valensi, with notes by Marie-Thérèse Blondeau (Paris: Gallimard, 2006), 2:989.

9. *The Plague*, 195.

10. *The Plague*, 271.

11. *The Plague*, 275.

12. *The Plague*, 301.

13. Fernand Bezançon and André Philibert, *Précis de pathologie médicale* (Paris: Masson, 1899). Cited in Albert Camus, *La peste*, in *Œuvres completes*, 2:1178.

14. *La peste*, in *Œuvres completes*, 2:1178.

15. Camus, *Carnets*, cahier 4, 989.

CHAPTER 12

1. J.-Ch. Jauffret, dir., *La guerre d'Algérie par les documents*, vol. 1, *L'avertissement, 1943–1946* (Vincennes: Service historique de l'armée de terre, 1990), 403.

2. Albert Camus, "Crisis in Algeria," May 13–14, 1945, in *Camus at "Combat": Writing, 1944–1947*, trans. Arthur Goldhammer (Princeton, NJ: Princeton University Press, 2006), 198–201. The article is the first in a series of six, gleaned in part from Camus's trip to Algeria, from April 18 to May 7 or 8. May 8, 1945, was the day of the veterans' march in Sétif.

3. Mohammed Harbi, "La guerre d'Algérie a commencé à Sétif," *Le monde diplomatique*, May 2005.

4. Henry Rousso, "L'épuration en France: Une histoire inachevée," *Vingtième siècle: Revue d'histoire* 33 (janvier–mars 1992): 78–105. Rousso estimates at 350,000 the number of cases sent to Courts of Justice and Civic Chambers, many of which were deemed unfounded and not pursued.

5. Albert Camus, *The Plague*, trans. Laura Marris (New York: Knopf, 2021), 330.

6. *The Plague*, 327.

7. *The Plague*, 328.

8. Albert Camus, "Outlaws," *Combat* (clandestine), April 1944, in *Camus at "Combat,"* 3–4.

9. "Justice and Charity," January 11, 1945, in *Camus at "Combat,"* 168–70.

10. Robert Brasillach, "Les sept internationales contre la patrie," *Je suis partout*, September 25, 1942.

11. Albert Camus to Marcel Aymé, January 27, 1945, in Albert Camus, *Œuvres complètes*, vol. 2 (Paris: Gallimard, 2005), 733–34.

12. Albert Camus, "L'incroyant et les chrétiens," lecture to the Dominicans in the Latour-Maubourg convent, 1948, in *Œuvres complètes*, 2:470–74.

13. Albert Camus, *Notebooks, 1942–1951*, trans. Justin O'Brien (New York: Knopf, 1965), 147.

14. Simone de Beauvoir, *Force of Circumstance*, trans. Richard Howard (New York: Putnam's, 1964), 22.

15. Description of the series by Camus, my translation from the Éditions Gallimard web page on Espoir: "*Collection* Espoir," Gallimard, http://www.gallimard.fr/Catalogue/GALLIMARD/Espoir, accessed November 3, 2021.

16. Robert Zaretsky has written beautiful books about both figures: on Camus, *Albert Camus: Elements of a Life* (Ithaca, NY: Cornell University Press, 2013) and *A Life Worth Living: Albert Camus and the Quest for Meaning* (Cambridge, MA: Harvard University Press, 2016); on Simone Weil, *The Subversive Simone Weil: A Life in Five Ideas* (Chicago: University of Chicago Press, 2020); and on their connection, "The Logic of the Rebel: On Simone Weil and Albert Camus," *Los Angeles Review of Books*, March 7, 2020, https://lareviewofbooks.org/article/logic-rebel-simone-weil-albert-camus/.

17. See Alice Kaplan, *The Collaborator: The Trial and Execution of Robert Brasillach* (Chicago: University of Chicago Press, 2000), esp. chaps. 9–11.

18. Nazism is described as a "scourge" or, in French, "un fléau" in "The Human Crisis" and "Time of the Murderers," in *Speaking Out: Lectures and Speeches, 1937–1950*, trans. Quintin Hoare (New York: Vintage, 2021).

19. *The Plague*, 331.

20. *The Plague*, 332. In the original: "les chambres, les caves, les malles, les mouchoirs et les paperasses." Albert Camus, *La peste* (Paris: Bibliothèque de la Pléiade, 2006), 2:248.

21. Henri Bourges, *La peste: Épidémiologie, bactériologie, prophylaxie* (Paris: Masson, 1899) and Bezançon and Philibert, *Précis de pathologie médicale*, quoted in Camus, *Œuvres complètes*, 2:1204.

22. Albert Camus, *The Rebel: An Essay on Man in Revolt*, trans. Anthony Bower (New York: Vintage, 1992), 181, edited.

CHAPTER 13

1. Albert Camus, *The Plague*, trans. Laura Marris (New York: Knopf, 2021), 68.

2. Olivier Todd, *Albert Camus: Une vie* (Paris: Gallimard, 1996), 63. This particular passage is not included in the abridged American edition in English translation.

3. For more on this phrase, see Alice's beautiful account in *Looking for "The Stranger": Albert Camus and the Life of a Literary Classic* (Chicago: University of Chicago Press, 2016), 92.

4. Albert Camus, *Notebooks, 1935–1942*, trans. Philip Thody (New York: Knopf, 1963), 3, edited.

5. "Problems of Latent Infection," *Journal of the American Medical Association* 103, no. 25 (December 1934): 1951–52.

6. See Anjuli Fatima Raza Kolb, *Epidemic Empire: Colonialism, Contagion, and Terror, 1817–2020* (Chicago: University of Chicago Press, 2020), 137.

7. *The Plague*, 17.

8. Letícia Parente, "Preparação II (1976)," Vimeo, uploaded 2014, https://vimeo.com/106547188.

9. *The Plague*, 271.

10. Quoted by Ronald Aronson, *Sartre and Camus: The Story of a Friendship and the Quarrel That Ended It* (Chicago: University of Chicago Press, 2004), 56.

11. "The Human Crisis," in *Speaking Out: Lectures and Speeches, 1937–1950*, trans. Quintin Hoare (New York: Vintage, 2021), forthcoming. This translation is from a 2016 performance of the speech at Columbia: "Albert Camus's 'The Human Crisis' read by Viggo Mortensen, 70 Years Later," YouTube, May 9, 2016, https://www.youtube.com/watch?v=aaFZJ_ymueA. This paragraph and the one that follows are adapted from my *New York Times* article, "Camus's Inoculation against Hate," April 16, 2020.

12. Romain Gary, introduction to *The Plague*, by Albert Camus, trans. Stuart Gilbert (New York: Time, Inc., 1962), xi–xii.

13. For more on the colonial history and power dynamics of plague serums, see

Aro Velmet, *Pasteur's Empire: Bacteriology and Politics in France, Its Colonies, and the World* (Oxford: Oxford University Press, 2020).

14. *The Plague*, 304.

15. Kathy High, *Blood Wars*, created by the Vampire Study Group, 2009–2010. Video trailer: http://vampirestudygroup.com/bloodwars/blood-stories/index.html.

16. David Carroll, *Albert Camus the Algerian* (New York: Columbia University Press, 2007), 55–56.

17. Jacqueline Rose, "Pointing the Finger," *London Review of Books* 45, no. 9 (May 7, 2020), https://www.lrb.co.uk/the-paper/v42/n09/jacqueline-rose/pointing-the-finger.

18. Albert Camus, "Letter to an Algerian Militant," *Algerian Chronicles*, ed. Alice Kaplan, trans. Arthur Goldhammer (Cambridge, MA: Harvard University Press, 2013), 113.

19. Albert Camus, *Exile and the Kingdom*, trans. Carol Cosman (New York: Vintage, 2006), 73.

20. Rose, "Pointing the Finger."

INDEX